AF394683

Ed. Cecily Chua, Labeja Kodua Okullu, Marta Michalowska

Putting money into concert halls, museums, or theatres seems obviously good for a city's or a nation's balance sheet; such investment attracts tourists who in turn activate a whole supply chain of activities, from restaurants and hotels to modest crafts flogging mementos. But this kind of tourist-orientated investment is not necessarily good for artists, and can indeed stifle the culture of a city.

It is news to no one that inequality is increasing in the global economy, in those places where economic growth has been intense. We usually think about such inequality in terms of the obscene amounts of capital controlled by those at the very top 1 or even .01 per cent. Meteoric expansion at the top has in the last thirty years been paralleled by income stagnation and declining social mobility in the middle or lower-middle classes.

Most artists are part of that stagnant middle. Of course, there is a global circuit of musicians and visual artists whose fortunes resemble those of Goldman Sachs bankers. Artists who live a more civic and modest existence have seen their fortunes decline in the last thirty years. A team of my students analysed a few years ago the economic condition of visual artists in New York City, finding a steady decline in income from the sale of their art, even as the incomes of the global-artist elite expanded almost exponentially; the number of shows in galleries for artists under thirty shrank by 40 per cent over a twenty-five-year period; rents on studio spaces tripled or quadrupled in the same period, forcing many artists to abandon the city in order to work.

These findings suggest there is a kind of zero-sum game at work in culture, just as in investment banking: what the elite gains, the mass loses. This zero-sum game has ruled, for instance, the city of Hamburg. It spent a decade and over €700 million on building the Elb-philharmonie concert hall, a vast project jutting out into the port of the city. The structure has successfully attracted tourists from around the world and global-brand musicians, but there's no money left in the city's coffers for support of youth orchestras, or for studios in which young artists can work, or for the semi-professional choirs which once fanned out over the Hanseatic North.

How can we get out of such a zero-sum game? To right the balance means investing more in producers and less on distributors. Moreover, we need to think about how to encourage communities of practitioners, not focus only on individual artists. The writer William Empson once declared 'the arts result from overcrowding', meaning that a community of people who do different things, speak in different voices, will interact, competing and conspiring, and so energise one another. This was the case in the early days of the tech revolution in places like Silicon Valley outside San Francisco or Nehru Place in Delhi. Such community building is the model we should follow in funding the arts.

But that alone cannot be the whole answer. When I chaired the urban studies committee at UNESCO, we pondered how investment in our World Heritage Sites could help them become tourist beacons while serving local communities. Our solution was partial: in places which required restoration, local artisans got the work, and the sites became places for educational programmes on history and heritage. But that doesn't grapple with the issue of building new or being big. Instead of the Elbphilharmonie model, how could a concert hall be designed for programmes small as well as big? How could it be integrated into the everyday working lives of artists in the city?

It is the same question to be put to big museums. Their 'public' should consist of makers as well as visitors: How can a museum service the needs of creators for the community? Creative work, like scientific research, entails a good deal of frustration and failure. How should we support – that is, invest in – this necessary dark side of the creative process?

Richard Sennett

This was the key question that sent Theatrum Mundi on an intellectual adventure in 2016, and through public events, workshops and roundtables, we built a discourse that brought together a diverse group of cultural producers across the UK, including choreographers, writers, architects and urbanists. These conversations gave rise to a multitude of questions exploring issues beyond the *concrete* infrastructure – the buildings where cultural activities happen – to consider the conditions that affect the way artists work. Our reaing of infrastructural conditions included organisational and management structures, the design and adaptation of workspaces, social and professional networks, funding mechanisms and planning regulations. To uncover these conditions, we looked at three broad forms of cultural production: *infrastructures of making*, including not only fine arts, crafts, construction and manufacture but also the production of everyday objects such as furniture, clothing and food; *infrastructures of perfomance*, considering dance, music, theatre and performance art, alongside practices engaging with speech, gestures and oral histories; and *infrastructures of the virtual*, including images, texts and designs that are usually produced and consumed via screens or as printed materials.

If we think of the public-facing cultural sites largely aimed at national and international tourists and visitors, such as monuments, museums, galleries and theatres, where culture is consumed and displayed as the 'urban stage', then its *behind-the-scenes* counterpart is the 'urban backstage', which includes both the *hidden* spaces where cultural production, experimentation and rehearsals take place and the underlying conditions that underpin these activities. The urban backstage is made up of invisible networks, relationships and labour that exist out of public view in our cities, producing 'everyday cultures' which are vital in fostering and cultivating a shared cultural identity and sense of belonging in our urban spaces.

From this provocation, the project Urban Backstages was born, a multi-year research programme spanning four cities: London, Glasgow, Marseille and Paris. In each of these cities, we spent about a month investigating sites of everyday cultural production. Our focus was, and is, personal, amplifying the voices, stories and experiences of artists, performers, makers, designers, craftspeople, fabricators, cafe owners and those running small businesses that support cultural production locally. We looked at their workspaces, ranging from repurposed factories to live-in work units, garages, purpose-built studios and converted railway arches. Our aim was to develop a broader account of the diversity of practices that generate the cultural life of the city, beyond traditional artist studios and artisanship, so we included light industry, digital production, materials suppliers and practices that may seem outside the scope of conventional understandings of culture such as hospitality and hairdressing, but which underpin cultural exchange and production, particularly within diasporic and working-class communities. We wanted to better understand the contribution small-scale producers make to the cultural life of the city and how the spaces they work in shape what they produce.

Throughout the project, in each of the four cities, we collected a large quantity of data in different forms, which we are making available to other researchers via a digital database: a repository of our findings, statistics, network diagrams, illustrations, maps, snippets of conversation, photographs and a film. The database can be accessed at backstages.city. At the same time, having spent three years observing and engaging with both people and places of everyday cultural production, we felt that each member of our team had something more to say than the database could accommodate. And from that sense of incompleteness, this book emerged, bringing together five essays where we question what culture in cities is, how it is *made*, where and under what conditions, and by whom. Each essay teases out stories, recipes, memories and shared moments of intimacy, proposing a different idea of what the uban backstage can be, based on the cultures of the everyday. The recurring themes of heritage, social value, visibility, flexibility and adaptability came to the surface as we put our thoughts and reflections into the first drafts of these essays. We

Introduction

present these as seeds of ideas towards making and sustaining shared forms of cultural life, where the image of the city emerges from the activity and cultural expressions of its inhabitants rather than being imposed by national, regional, citywide, or local policies and plans developed by public and private bodies and authorities.

The first essay in this book – *"The Sensorial as Infrastructure: Making Pandebono"* by Andrea Cetrulo, Elahe Karimnia, and John Bingham-Hall – borrows the recipe for pandebono, a traditional Colombian pastry, and uses it as both a portal to a faraway home and a tool for dealing with uprootedness, homesickness and alienation. The pandebono becomes a recipe for survival, its changing ingredients telling a story of migration, resourcefulness and adaptability.

"The Medusa effect" by Cecily Chua takes a narrative *dérive* through the Barras Market in Glasgow, drawing on stories from the market traders and makers who have lived and worked there for decades, resisting the decline and regeneration of their neighbourhood. The essay argues for a new definition of what 'cultural heritage' can be.

"Flexibility in Cultural Production" by Elahe Karimnia interrogates different readings of what flexibility is and can be, beyond a buzzword linked to creative co-working spaces. It focuses on what flexibility means to cultural producers, particularly those whose practices exist at the margins, too noisy, messy or movement based to fit neatly into the sanitised co-working environments where creativity rarely ventures beyond the computer screen.

"Invisible Cities" by Fani Kostourou unfolds as a *flâneuse* account of two cities – London and Paris – proposing a comparative reflection on the role of architecture and urban design production and policies in the neighbourhoods of Elephant and Castle, London, and La Goutte d'Or, Paris. It reveals the invisible networks and infrastructures supporting creative communities, workspaces, and local economies, uncovering lessons one city can learn from another.

We end the book with *"What's the Worth of It All?"*: by John Bingham-Hall, which explores the value of culture from different perspectives and applies different scales from central government to individual cultural producers –the protagonists of this essay – that make and maintain the urban backstage.

And without further ado, we invite you to enter the backstage – the urban backstage.

Cecily Chua, Labeja Kodua Okullu, Marta Michalowska

Acknowledgements Urban Backstages would not be possible without funding from the Axel and Margaret Ax:son Johnson Foundation and Kungliga Tekniska Högskolan (KTH) Centre for the Future of Places in Stockholm. We would like to thank Peter Elmlund, Director for Urban City Research at the Ax:son Johnson Foundation, projects leader Morgane Schwab, and Tigran Haas, Professor of Urban Design and Planning at KTH, for their generous support of this project and the many conversations we had with them which helped shape the focus of our research.

We would like to thank Marcos Villalba and Santiago Confalonieri for their intelligent, intuitive and decisive design. We would like to thank the research team – Andrea Cetrulo, Cecily Chua, Elahe Karimnia, Fani Kostourou, John Bingham-Hall and Justinien Tribillon – for their dedication, imagination, and tenacity in undertaking the fieldwork as an engine to craft these essays. We would like to thank Imogen Free and Sriwhana Spong for their meticulous and rigorous proofreading.

Last but not least, we would like to thank all of the people we interviewed as part of this project across London, Glasgow, Paris and Marseille, who welcomed us into their workspaces and generously shared their time, experience and works in progress that brought new thinking and ideas to the fore.

The Sensorial as Infrastructure: Making Pandebono

Andrea Cetrulo, Elahe Karimnia, John Bingham-Hall

During one of our visits to Andrés and Valentina at La Caleñita, the café they've been running for nine years in one of the adapted railway arches at Elephant and Castle in South London, we were greeted with a coffee accompanied by a soft, warm, cloudy, savoury sphere-like bread, known in their native Colombia as pandebono. It was meant to be accepted as an act of generosity and hospitality in the vein of Marcel Mauss's idea of the gift, a form of exchange underpinning the formation of alliances and solidarity beyond self-interest.[1] It is through these dynamics of altruistic reciprocal relationships that La Caleñita operates on a daily basis.

Recipe as knowledge infrastructure

The etymology of the bread in question is somewhat of a mystery, yet the most commonly accepted version is that it derives from the Spanish words *pan* (bread) and *de* (of) and *bono* (from buono, Italian for 'good'), attributed to an Italian baker who used to sell the pastry on the streets of Cali, chanting 'pan del buono!'. Another version is that it was named after the Finca El Bono, an eighteenth-century rural stately home in the small town of Valle del Cauca, in Cali, where the bread originated and was sold.

The mythology and folklore surrounding its origins encompass a sort of syncretism that is reflected in the ingredients themselves: blending yuca (or cassava) and corn, both autochthonous to South America; cheese and butter made with cow's milk, introduced to the Americas by European colonisers; and the artisanry of the Italian immigrants of Cali who allegedly initiated its production. Pandebono is often accompanied by *dulce de guayaba* (guava jam) and a cup of hot chocolate, both tropical fruits that, as Gabriel Garcia-Márquez wrote in *The Fragrance of Guava* (1982),[2] evoke memories of his childhood and permeate the imagination through their very smell. Smell as memory. Texture as memory. Vivid, tangible, yet somehow intangible in the imagination. A glutinous dough that agglutinates individuals from diverse Latin American countries in a faraway city and acts as an infrastructure for sustaining everyday life. The amulet of the nomad, embodying both displacement and persistence at the same time.

When Valentina was prompted to share her recipe, she smiled and said, 'Pandebono is something that I relate to that time of the day in the afternoon before late dinner. I always had it at my home after school.'

Pandebono ingredients:

- Almidón de yuca
- Harina de maíz
- Huevos
- Queso costeño
- Mantequilla
- Levadura

Valentina describes her process:

1. Mix all the ingredients
2. Grate the cheese finely
3. Knead
4. Form bollos in your hands
5. Make a hole
6. Preheat the oven to 190 degrees
7. Leave it in for 15 minutes (or so) until … you know …
8. Tacit knowledge reigns. When it's ready, you should 'feel' it. Don't overthink it.
9. Bake until golden.

The way the recipe is enunciated is in the manner of an oral culture. Or alternately, a manual or embodied culture, like that of the craftswoman who performs the task with mastery, yet also with an over-familiarity

1   Mauss, M. (1925.) *The Gift: The Form and Reason for Exchange in Archaic Societies.* Reprint, 1954.
2   García Márquez, G. and Mendoza, P. (1982) *The Fragrance of Guava.*

Andrea Cetrulo, John Bingham-Hall, Elahe Karimnia

with the object at hand that makes it hard for her to rationalize the process and put it into words: '[it is] a process essential to all skills, the conversion of information and practices into tacit knowledge',[3] and 'what you know may be so familiar to you that you might take for granted its touchstone references, assuming that others have identical touchstones'.[4]

Improvised adaptations   Although this recipe travels with its makers as a kind of cultural heritage – already stabilised in form – it becomes the basis for improvisation when relocated from Cali to London, necessarily so. In Andrés's words: 'You don't find all the necessary ingredients here… Everything here tastes very different!' Like other restaurants forming the Latin American cultural hub nested in the railway arches of Maldonado Walk, Andrés and Valentina source many of their goods from the neighbouring shop La Chatica, which specializes in importing regional products. But they must also resort to stand-in ingredients from the British supermarket chain TESCO, like the ersatz queso costeño, mimicked by the more readily-available feta cheese, or indeed, 'Greek-style salad cheese' – a simulacrum of one immigrant food masquerading as another.

The import of certain Latin American animal products has been banned due to health and safety regulations in the United Kingdom.[5] As a remedy, La Chatica (registered as La Casa de Jack Ltd.) sells its own line of products that resemble the 'real thing'. Other delicacies, such as dulce de guayaba, are imported directly from Colombia in big batches and then repackaged in small quantities for sale in shops across Europe. Ingredients that are not produced in London are distributed and exported from Spain, an important Latin American migration node in the past three decades. The Spain-United Kingdom connection has been reinforced since the 2008 crisis when migrants relocated from Southern European countries to London, perceived as a better place for economic prosperity.

In London, one of the most popular food brands amongst Latin immigrants is Sol Andino, a Peruvian-owned Business with an online store and a high street location on Old Kent Road in South London, a spot where Latin migrants live and gather. Sol Andino is one of the biggest distributors, catering to several shops and restaurants in the city. These kinds of networks of specialist food supply and consumption produce and reproduce this area of South London, stretching from Kennington to Old Kent Road via Elephant and Castle, as a zone of Latin American culture. Unlike the specialist coffee joints of the aspirational middle classes (which no one knows exactly how to define but everyone can instantly recognise), this particular entanglement of food, culture, and socio-economics is focused around ingredients available in particular locations, rather than aesthetics which can be reproduced anywhere.

Queso costeño, a soft, salty cow's milk cheese originating from the Caribbean coast of Colombia and a key ingredient in pandebono, is also made in-house by Andrés and Valentina themselves, which allows them to cut costs compared to buying it ready-made: 'The queso that you find here doesn't even come close to the one from Colombia'. In their café, this improvisation is also evident in the construction of the space itself. A railway arch, emblematic of a very Victorian, very British kind of progress, is reconfigured as a mini ecosystem of Latin businesses, from money transfer to the making of clothes

and the making of pandebono. A lead tenant renting directly from the landlord – once the public Network Rail but now the private 'Arch Company' – has created sublettable units through simple plywood partitions, which have in turn been adapted by their own tenants for

3   Sennett, R. (2008) *The Craftsman.*
4   Ibid.
5   *Importing live animals, animal products and high-risk food and feed not of animal origin from non-EU countries to Great Britain* (2015). [gov.uk/guidance/importing-live-animals-or-animal-products-fromnon-eu-countries].

    The Sensorial as Infrastructure: Making Pandebono

a multitude of uses. What makes this place 'Latin American', or in La Caleñita's case, Colombian? Language, smells, tastes, sounds from the TV. Things that cannot be made through architecture but through use. However, it is not only the sensorial environment that constitutes a cultural space, but the way of producing it.

• Take a blank railway arch
• Provide cheap rent
• Adapt the space for basic needs and desires with simple materials
• Allow basic sub-divisions to be made without requiring permissions
• Allow subtenants to add the finishing touches

A recipe for coping   Informality and self-reliance have travelled in the bodies of people like Andrés and Valentina, another unwritten recipe allowing local spatial ingredients to be recooked into something distinct and culturally enriching. As a La Caleñita habitué puts it, '[Pandebono] brings memories of driving to the outskirts of Bogotá to have it on Sundays with my family when I was a child. It's like you need to know it. Visually it's not appealing; you need to feel it. I personally love the warmth and elasticity of it.' Another customer from Chile, new to the place, inquires about the different baked goods displayed on the counter at La Caleñita, unsure of which one to pick: 'I am Chilean, but there are so many commonalities between Latin Americans anyways, it feels like home.' These often unspoken, shared codes are held together by what Benedict Anderson coined 'imagined communities',[6] the idea of a Pan Latin American community based on affinity brought by the peculiar needs of relocation and infrastructures of coping.

In Andrés's words: 'This place acts as a social hub, not only a restaurant. When a new migrant [from Latin America] arrives with just a suitcase and nowhere to go, we provide them with food and shelter. This pays back, as they always return once their situation gets better.' Pandebono fulfils a social function and enhances the power of imaginations through the sensorial, acting as a pillar for coping with the vicissitudes of instability. When it's consumed, it elicits memories of place, bringing to mind that 'all really inhabited space bears the essence of the notion of home'.[7]

Coping is a creative act, an improvisational activity, an attitude towards the world of uncertainties, focussing on opportunities, and forging solidarity. Migrants coping with structured inequalities in everyday life highlight their creative and experimental performance as they go; no matter that Andrés and Valentina can't get the same ingredients for pandebono in London, they are confident in themselves and their community for finding alternative resources and mutual support. Pandebono cannot be simply reduced to a recipe of ingredients, like those attempts at formulating context-free suggestions for the problems our cities deal with. The recipe, rather than a prescriptive form, becomes  support for a kind of improvisation that allows the immigrant to reconfigure the unfamiliar materials of the host country into an embodiment of home. It is an organising framework that allows unrelated elements – Greek-style salad cheese, yucca, British eggs – to participate in the construction of something not constituted by any one of them individually but by their relationships.

Cooking and infrastructuring   What do we learn from pandebono, then, about culture and its infrastructure, the conditions that enable those without institutional or political power to make and remake the city? Like recipes, infrastructures can be used to enable or to constrain. If they fix a set of predefined elements

6   Anderson, B. (1983) *Imagined Communities.* Reprint, Verso, 2006.
7   Bachelard, G. (1958) *The Poetics of Space.*

Andrea Cetrulo, John Bingham-Hall, Elahe Karimnia

so rigidly that the malfunctioning or unavailability of one of them invalidates the whole structure, they bring about situations of control and redundancy. We can think of 'recipes' for cultural regeneration in the Bilbao model, built around a 'flagship' museum, preconceived from building to programme. If the museum does not work, both itself and its surrounding 'cultural district' can become deserted wastelands, unable to be rethought and readapted from the bottom up by virtue of being designed for institutional-scale actors. Like the proverbial soufflé in which one failure renders the whole thing useless, such masterplanning is what Sennett calls 'closed' or 'complete form'.[8] Alternately, recipes can be 'open forms', organising frameworks choreographing a set of relationships between interchangeable elements, a way of passing on ideas and methods for making form with the materials to hand. This points to a different kind of cultural planning in which a broad set of infrastructures are understood, and individuals and small collectivities make their own forms of cultural space, which then become infrastructures for other things, like sensing and coping.

For Andrés and Valentina, and other members of their community, improvisation is essential when working with this lack of an overarching plan or institutional structure – in a state of 'unincorporation'[9] – and without the imposition of a 'design' that predetermines the aesthetic end-point. This is evident in the social support structures that have emerged around the informally adapted infrastructure of the arches on Maldonado Walk.

Improvisation is helping to find last-minute accommodation for newcomers, or covering shifts with short notice, or assisting each other with moving house, or setting up an impromptu shelter in the kitchen for anyone who needs it. Improvisation is plastering the wall of a dim, austere cave-like structure under a railway station with the picture of a tropical beach, feeding not only the stomachs but also the imaginations of those who gather here. But improvisation does not happen in a vacuum. As scores can provide a shared basis on top of which performers improvise with sound and movement,[10] infrastructural recipes made of knowledge, space, material, and planning policy are the solid ground that enables immigrant makers to improvise with and gain agency over urban form.

Despite the undeniable power that comes with the migrant's ability to reconstruct, remodel, and reshape new microcosms for herself and others around her, recent regeneration strategies for the area, which include the imminent sale of the railway arches to private investors, threaten the continuity of these accessible spaces for the production of goods and immaterial affective support structures. Where there is a strong reliance on the space of place, can a place like this be swept away in its materiality without dragging with it the lifeworld of those who inhabit it?

8   Sennett, R. (2019) *Building and Dwelling.*
9   Bingham-Hall, J., Chua, C., Cetrulo, A., and Ali, J. (2019) *Urban Backstages: Unincorporated Artists Unite.*
10   Bingham-Hall, J. (2019) "What kind of thing is a score?" [theatrum-mundi.org/library/what-kind-of-thing-is-a-score/].

The Sensorial as Infrastructure: Making Pandebono

The Medusa Effect

Cecily Chua

It is a hot and humid afternoon on the day we head to The Barras in Glasgow's East End neighbourhood of Calton, home to the city's oldest and largest street and indoor market. It is the height of Scottish summer, when long evenings stretch late into the night. But we are not here on a city break, exploring the less touristic sites Glasgow has to offer. We are urban researchers, here to find the parts of the city where culture is conceived and shaped, whilst hidden from the public eye. As we walk, a teenage boy peddles languidly up and down the quiet street on a mauve children's bicycle. Back and forth he goes, past the iconic Barrowland Ballroom's star-spangled neon sign. He calls to passers-by, offering to sell the bicycle for ten pounds, then five pounds, or even four.

At the Barras, we meet Barry, the fourth-generation marketeer, as he rolls up the corrugated metal shutter of the Barras East End Studios (BEES). Part makers' space, part market, BEES is a ramshackle assembly of interconnected warehouses huddled between two ornate Victorian factory buildings. It is one of the last clusters of marketeers still operating in the Barras amid vacant shop fronts and windowless storage buildings. We approach a squat one-story brick building with a well-worn corrugated tin roof animated by a large hand-painted mural which Barry says is their crest. The spidery black line drawing features a beehive, three threatening cats playing harmonicas, and a fish hovering in front of a mushroom cloud. Barry is reticent to explain the crest's symbolism to us but tells us that the name of the space was chosen as a tongue-in-cheek reference to Glasgow's Workshop & Artists Studio Provision Scotland (WASPS), Scotland's premier provider of creative studio spaces, which currently houses around a thousand artists and organisations.[1] He tells us, 'We're the BEES, and they're the WASPS. But the WASPS have got all the money, right?'

The cavernous maze of spaces inside BEES feels a world away from the studios offered by WASPS in a former ironworks just five minutes up the road. The spaces at WASPS have freshly painted white walls, with sunlight spilling from generous windows, and come fully equipped with lighting, heating and Wi-Fi. In contrast, the light is murky within the windowless interior of BEES, where an assortment of sixteen corrugated metal stalls in various stages of construction are arranged around an L-shaped central space. We skirt around the headless torso of a mannequin, between stacks of paintings in gilded frames and piles of mismatched crockery. But amongst the jumble of objects, furniture, and household detritus is a hive of creative production. Each unit doubles as both workshop and shopfront, where traders make and sell handmade clothes, children's toys, and repurposed furniture. At BEES, the prices of goods, as well as rents, are negotiable and the opening hours flexible. Some of the goods on offer might appear to have a shady provenance if one were to take Barry's word at face value when he winks and says that they may have 'fallen from the back of a lorry'.

A few metres on, we hear the rhythmic hum of a sewing machine and meet Nicky, a milliner working in a space with walls lined with richly patterned Turkish rugs. 'I'm a magpie', she says, as she sews peacock feathers onto a crimson felt hat, 'always on the lookout for scraps of pretty things. I make use of things most people would consider junk.' Opposite Nicky's unit is a zero-waste café run by Lina. The smell of freshly baked bread lures us towards a hatch in the wall through which Lina, balancing a baby on her hip, sells homemade scones daubed with jam and cream, ice lollies and lemonade. We buy a strawberry lolly and move onwards, our mouths numbed by the sweet ice.

1 WASPS. (2022) "About", [https://www.WASPSstudios.org.uk/about].

Cecily Chua

In the next unit we meet Mairi, a former teacher who had to retire due to bouts of ill health. Her furniture upcycling business has given her a second chance at a career on her own terms. She tells us: 'Everyone deserves a second chance and so should preloved furniture, so that's what I do.' Behind half-closed roller shutters, she paints a battered old rocking horse in white, gold and cerulean. A self-confessed 'hoarder', she has a deep affection for the Barras, and visiting the market was part of her childhood Saturday morning ritual. 'I used to come with my mum and my nana when I was a wee girl,' she says.

She describes to us how the owners of BEES, Barry and Danny, will go out of their way to help. They have assisted her in painting and carpeting her space and have provided a shared tool library that allows her to make the alterations she needs to vintage furniture pieces with no added cost. She pats a large teak chest; its cherry-coloured wood is covered with marks and ridges, reminiscent of a landscape seen from above. With pride, she says, 'Real carpenters have made this – not machines – real people. It's got all these stories behind it; you can feel that it's been through a lot.' Perhaps this chest is a metaphor for the building itself, a place that has passed through many hands. Parts have been added and demolished, and trading families have come and gone through the generations. BEES is a well-worn but well-loved space, a little down at heel but with a rich patina of stories and relationships that have built up over time.

We return to the Wee Cafe, where Lina has laid out an assortment of cakes and pastries on the counter. She tells us that she worked as a sous-chef in several high-end kitchens in Glasgow before taking maternity leave. She explains that working at BEES has helped

her get back into employment, as she can take things at her own pace. 'If I'm not feeling like I have to be open at ten, I'm opening at eleven,' she says. The freedom that a space like BEES offers her could not be found in most fast-paced, professional kitchens, where shifts and opening times are set. Here, she has the flexibility to balance running a business alongside taking care of two young children. At the Barras, away from the hustle and bustle of Glasgow's merchant centre, things follow their own rhythm. She tells us that at BEES, goods and services are often exchanged instead of money. A frequent customer who does odd jobs fixed Lina's pipes, and in exchange they often pop in for a free cup of coffee. They call this 'the Barras way', a term which is elastic enough to encompass different rituals, jokes, and informal transactions that together form infrastructures of mutual need that help to create a sense of belonging and shared identity for the space.

At BEES, tactics such as buying, selling, bartering, gossiping, and cooking form the tools of an informal market economy which are used by its inhabitants to transform an appropriate space, often circumventing, or in resistance to, the way of life imposed by authorities. Spaces like BEES provide the opportunity for such practices to take place, satirising everyday life by presenting extremes of cultural experience. It is in this respect that they serve as an active rather than passive monument to the way we live our lives. It is not its architectural fabric that defines the value of this space but the myriad of sensorial experiences and exchanges that take place here.

On tarot and dreaming   In a darkened nook at the back of the room, a gauzy banner advertises the services of 'Laura with the Aura', a clairvoyant whose family has deep roots in the market, where she has been offering tarot readings for the past six decades. With a raised hand, she silently beckons us into her space, the sounds from outside dampened by velvet drapes. We watch as a set of well-worn cards are shuffled through hands embellished with silver rings. Within the deck, secret histories and ceremonial magic are folded. Do these cards tell the future or hold the past? She tells us they have been passed down through the hands of many generations of women, holding court over births, marriages and deaths. Each card is a talisman, a character that only the tarot reader herself can reveal, but together they tell the interconnected stories of a neighbourhood. She asks us each to pull a card through which she will conjure a brief history of the Barras.

† *The High Priestess, the Barras Queen, reigns over the market come rain, wind or shine.*

She is the divinity of the mercantile spirit; the traders leave offerings to win her favour: barrows overflowing with apples, bread, milk and dusky-eyed potatoes. A dynasty of marketeers whose ancestors came off the boats with only the shirts off their backs to sell.

The Barras Queen is their patron saint, a guiding light and an amulet against the grinding cold, relentless rain and the dull ache of hunger. She is the comfort of a candlelit shelter, a dram of whisky or a pot of stew on the stove.

‡ *The Magician, a trickster, enchanter and savant, finds his form as a band leader in a smoke-filled ballroom. Rocking back on his heels, he conducts a swaggering swing of horns and a snap and crash of cymbals. Eyes closed tight in reverie, he guides the deep bass notes, which widen and open into black and blue shadows.*

On the dancefloor, The Lovers trip the light fantastic, holding each other, seeing stars. They don't know yet that their time together will be short, soon to be interrupted by the looming spectre of war in a cold, far-off land. They will only have this moment and the sweet nothings whispered between the jitterbug and the Charleston jive.

Is it possible to recognise the importance of rituals, aural traditions, folklore and legends as important tools to record and share our collective memories? Tarot and clairvoyance are ancient arts, part of the reproduction of symbolism and myths that store ideas about shared life that date back to the fifteenth century. They are tools to open a space for dreaming, magic and storytelling, tools that have been made blunt and unwieldy in our logocentric society, where productivity in cultural spaces needs to be quantified to be valued. Whilst tarot is clearly 'cultural' in this way, and though it involves the exchange of money for skills, it is difficult to imagine it mapped as part of public sector-led research on cultural industries and their infrastructures. Ancient practices such as tarot reading are offered a refuge in spaces like BEES, where mutual reliance is necessary, and solidarities can flourish between the commercial, the industrial, and the occult.

On the dangers of nostalgia   The apocalyptic emptiness of the Barras makes it a popular filming location for dystopian films and TV productions.[2] Now well past its heyday, the market echoes Glasgow's well-trodden narrative of post-industrial decline following the collapse of heavy industry along the River Clyde in the post-WWII period. In Calton, the combined damage of slum clearances in the 1970s, the obsolescence of its industry (brickworks, textile and metal forges), and the decline of the market has resulted in a district that scores high on multiple measures of deprivation, with 42.9% of children living in poverty, and 23.7% of its residents claiming out-of-work benefits in 2020.[3] In the mid-2000s, the district had the lowest life expectancy in the United Kingdom.[4] In the past ten years, a range of new arts and music initiatives have been introduced to support the East End communities, including creative

† THE BARRAS QUEEN: During the nineteenth century, the Barras was once one of Glasgow's most densely built-up areas of tenements, civic buildings, and factories. Founded at the beginning of the twentieth century by local entrepreneur Maggie McIver, the market sprang up from within this hive of activity, and many of its initial traders were Irish immigrants who arrived via boat, en masse and in several waves, at the Broomielaw on the River Clyde.

A formidable widow and mother of nine, she was dubbed the Barras Queen, becoming the de facto leader and vanguard of the market. The Barras provided a vital lifeline for recent migrants, a first foothold to gain economic stability on arrival.

‡ THE MAGICIAN: By 1926, McIver had created a covered market to further establish the rights of market traders and established the Barrowland Ballroom as a recreational space for the traders, which is still open today as a legendary music venue. Its star-spangled sign is part of the visual iconography of the city and often the first thing people mentioned in various arts spaces, venues, and bars across the city, when we told them we were conducting research in the Barras.

When the ballroom originally opened, it had its own resident jazz band, Billy Macgregor and the Gaybirds. It became so popular with servicemen during WWII that it was even mentioned as a target in one of William Joyce's propaganda broadcasts on behalf of the Nazis.

2   Anon. (2018) "Scottish landmarks transformed into blood-soaked battle-zones for new zombie flick", *Daily Record* [https://www.dailyrecord.co.uk/news/scottish-news/gallery/scottish-landmarks-transformed-blood-soaked-1332756].
3   Scottish Government (2020) *Scottish Index of Multiple Deprivation* [https://simd.scot/#/simd2020/BTTTFTT/9/-4.0000/55.9000].
4   Walsh, D. (2016) "History, politics and vulnerability: explaining excess mortality" [https://www.gcph.co.uk/publications/635_hist ory_politics_and_vulnerability_explaining_excess_mortality]

Cecily Chua

workspaces such as Many Studios and Glasgow Collective, and music venues such as Saint Luke's and The Space. However, this process has happened slowly and incrementally due to the piecemeal land ownership of the building stock of the Barras, much of it spread between the descendants of the historic marketeering families. This has meant it has been impossible for developers to buy up large swathes of land. Thus, the Barras is currently caught in a twilight zone between decline and regeneration, a state of temporary equilibrium where newer initiatives and existing traders can seemingly coexist. Urban researcher Pablo Arboleda writes in his essay *"Notes from a shrinking market"* (2020) that the market has so far eluded the typical urban regeneration narrative prevalent in other areas of the city.[5] For example, nearby Govanhill is the perfect microcosm of creative interest, cheap rent and a socio-economically diverse demographic, making it an attractive neighbourhood for artists and makers and, subsequently, a desirable asset for commercial developers.

Thus, current stasis of the Barras creates an opportunity to reconsider its heritage value from the perspective of social preservation, before its old guard of traders has completely disappeared. Could a more nuanced understanding of what is defined as 'cultural heritage' influence its future regeneration in a more democratic and inclusive fashion? Whilst some of the market's architectural heritage has been recognised by the local authority through the listing of several notable buildings, the recent approach to the intangible cultural heritage of the Barras has been to present a sanitised history of the market. The Barras 100 was a year-long arts and heritage centenary programme initiated in 2021 and funded by Glasgow City Council, Creative Scotland and Glasgow City Heritage Trust. A large portion of the funding for the event went towards a permanent exhibition of black-and-white photographs of the market. We spoke to the architect and studio manager of Many Studios, one of the newer gallery

and creative workspace initiatives in the Barras. He told us, in his experience of working with the council 'there was a desire to fetishize that heritage but not support the actual economic or entrepreneurial aspect of it by actively creating policies and structures. This meant that the people who had been working here for a long time were beginning to get more and more disenfranchised.'

This focus on sentiment and nostalgia seeks to preserve – or freeze – the character of a place as a fixed, fetishised artefact, rather than understanding that a vital part of its identity is the live pattern of usage, the interaction between traders, visitors, makers, and the social bonds that happen within and around it. Presenting the history of the Barras as a linear timeline of frictionless black-and-white photographs posits the site's 'heritage' as an idealised museum of its former self. The council's approach could be compared to *the Medusa effect*, fossilising the people who have built this legacy rather than supporting them to continue their practices.

The forming of the Barras Market itself was not a frictionless process. Established by Irish migrants at the turn of the twentieth century, it was a site founded on contestation, civil disobedience, and grassroots rebellion against urban legislation, and these processes have often overlapped with informal and sometimes criminal activities. In 1921, when the district council attempted to shut down its activities – penalising and charging street traders – local entrepreneur, Maggie McIver, made it her mission to legitimise the market. She achieved this by starting a business, renting out over 300 barrows to local hawkers in her yard in Marshall Lane in order to give traders a registered address.[6]

5   Arboleda, P. (2020) "Notes from a shrinking market 'Anticipatory nostalgia' and place-making in the midst of change" in M.A. Rhodes II, W.R. Price, A. Walker (eds.). *Geographies of Post-Industrial Place, Memory, and Heritage*, pp. 23–36.

6   Naughton, N. (2014) *Glasgow's East End: A Social History: From Bishop to Barraboys*, p. 253.

The uneasy relationship between market traders and the local authority has persisted into the present day. Barry tells us about how, in 2009, Glasgow City Council ordered the much-protested closure of the nearby Paddy's Market, described by locals as the Barras Market's little sister. Named for the influx of Irish migrants who made up its traders and clientele, Paddy's had a controversial reputation and was famously declared by councillor George Ryan a 'crime-ridden midden'[7] due to its links with organised crime and Calton's opioid crisis. In protest against its closure, the traders of Paddy's dressed in black and staged a funeral procession to the City Chambers, a performance complete with a coffin to symbolise the literal death of the market. Journalist Lorna Martin reported on the market's demise in *The Guardian*: 'To describe the forty or so traders affected, some of whom have been there for seventy years, as upset and angry is an understatement. They say the market is a unique piece of the city's heritage.'[8]

The actions taken by Glasgow City Council could be described as what economic geographer David Harvey terms 'creative destruction', a type of urban restructuring where architecture becomes commodified and the death of a specific architecture or space symbolises progress. Harvey notes that 'this nearly always has a class dimension, since it is usually the poor, the underprivileged, and those marginalised from political power that suffer first and foremost from this process'.[9] Plans for a 'new vision' to revitalise the area and lease the market units to artists and 'legitimate traders' have, as of yet, failed to materialise. The site is still derelict over a decade later. The fate of Paddy's Market remains an ominous warning, perhaps foreshadowing the future of the Barras.

Who gets to decide what a city's cultural heritage is? Who is involved in the decision-making? And who is left out? Despite its current dwindling footfall, the Barras Market still looms large in the public imagination as an iconic part of the city's mythology (mentioned in many tourist guides as an authentic Glaswegian experience), and depictions of the market often veer between sentimentality and condemnation.[10] According to headlines in the *Glasgow Times* and *The Scotsman*, the market is a hotbed of crime and illegal activity with a history of gang violence and organised crime.[11] However, traders like Barry, part of the market's old guard, describe the Barras in hallowed tones as a celebrated autonomous realm of grassroots resilience and economic independence for the urban working classes. These conflicting and mythic depictions of the market create binary narratives that overshadow the struggles and realities of many of the traders who are still trying to make a living operating here. As McIver's historic interventions have demonstrated, the formalisation and legitimisation of certain cultural practices, particularly migrant and working-class activities, is often hard-won.

On heritage beyond eulogy

Back at BEES, the sun is setting, and the squeak and rattle of the roller shutters signal closing time. We join a small group of people who have gathered outside on an assortment of stools, mismatched chairs, and an old sofa. Resident artist Rory, Sage of the Clyde, is here in his paint-splattered fur coat and a bowler hat with several pairs of sunglasses perched on top. We pass around a bottle of whisky whilst enjoying some dense and fruity Dundee cake left over from Lina's Café. Someone is singing a Gaelic folk song with a low and wistful melody whilst two small children take it in turns to don a vampire mask and chase one another. We wonder if the glow in our cheeks is from the whisky, the song or the late evening sunshine. Whisky in

7   Martin, L. (2019) "Glasgow bids farewell to Paddy's Market", *The Guardian* [https://www.theguardian.com/uk/2009/may/14/paddys-market-closure-glasgow-scotland?mobile-redirect=false].

8   Ibid.

9   Harvey, D. (2013) *Rebel Cities: From the Right to the City to the Urban Revolution*, p. 139.

10 Holmes, J. (2018) "A Perfect Day in Glasgow", *Timeout* [https://www.timeout.com/glasgow/things-to-do/a-perfect-day-in-glasgow].

11 Patterson, S. (2014) "Dozens of people charged over counterfeit goods at Barras", *Glasgow Times* [https://www.glasgowtimes.co.uk/news/13295925.dozens-of-people-charged-over-counterfeit-goods-at-barras].

Cecily Chua

hand, Barry reflects on his determination to establish BEES as a creative community, recognising the stagnation and obsolescence of many of the traditional traders still operating in the market, selling outdated technology like CRT TVs, DVDs, SCART leads, VHS. Recognising the success of newer arts initiatives as part of the area's cultural regeneration, he was adamant that everyone he rents space to in BEES should have a craft or make things on the premises. 'I know it's quite rustic and boho-chic here still, but we're on our way,' he says jovially.

Barry's repositioning of BEES as a creative workspace echoes McIver's historic interventions to protect and legitimise the market, reinventing and repackaging existing practices to make them fit within the trends of current urban planning rhetoric. BEES demonstrates how in the face of adversity, cooperative infrastructures can form based on mutual need. However, it is important not to romanticise the circumstances in which such infrastructures arise. Prior to the pandemic, mutual aid networks occurred extensively in marginalised communities in urban working-class areas, often in reaction to desperate need due to a lack of state-led provision and social and political exclusion. Often the types of cultural production happening within these communities goes unrecognized by city authorities as valid forms of culture or heritage. This is in part because their informality makes them hard to categorise, and thus they don't fit easily into a formally recognised market-driven definition of the creative industries: fashion, architecture, fine art and so on. Without much start-up capital and investment, or support from the public funding that some of its more agile neighbours have been able to access, BEES is a fragile infrastructure, dependent solely on the cooperation and solidarity of its members.

What is needed is an approach to heritage that eschews nostalgia for the past and challenges the Medusa effect: the freezing of places into relics of their former selves. Spaces like BEES demonstrate an alternative tool kit for survival, forged through the mutual support of a community that has overcome many combined challenges. They provide a refuge for forms of cultural production that often go unrecognised in the formal rhetoric of planning for culture. People cannot be taken out of the equation, as they are just as important to the identity of a place as the material landscape and physical infrastructures. To create resilient and democratic urban spaces and communities, we need to embrace the fact that conflict and mediation are often necessary agents in the making of places. We need to look beyond the narrow definitions of what constitutes culture in planning to include the contributions of migrant and working-class communities and support types of making and storytelling that are vital to the identity of a place. We need to provide a framework and support for cultural producers like those at BEES to continue to make and maintain their own infrastructures. Glasgow City Council's famous slogan 'People Make Glasgow' has never been truer than in the Barras, a living, breathing tableau of the city's cultural heritage.

Flexibility in Cultural Production

Elahe Karimnia

Flexibility, in the context of contemporary creative industries, has become a glamorised phenomenon, a buzzword used to illustrate an ideal working condition for cultural producers. The growth in, use of flexibility as a concept in urban discourse must be discussed in relation to the birth of *creative industry* and *creative class* in cities.[1] Since the late 1990s, and particularly within the last decade, neoliberal policymakers have started to highlight their openness and willingness to accommodate creative industries,[2] through various strategies and at different scales,[3] as a means to instigate economic growth and increase competitiveness.[4] The types of cultural production that are considered part of the creative industries illustrate a polarised debate. Modern (neoliberal) capitalism has co-opted the idea of creativity, so that almost any desk-based job could be reframed as creative. This system expects workers to be flexible and to adapt to hostile and precarious working environments by promoting profit-driven individualism. Practices which might not fit into this sector-based, market-driven definition of the creative class, such as craftspeople, performers and industrial makers, often find adequate, affordable workspace difficult to obtain.

In the world of architecture, this notion of flexibility manifests itself in the design of co-working spaces, marketed as spaces for creativity and freedom. The trend of co-working spaces sweeping cities around the world targets vacant, predominantly post-industrial buildings for adaptive reuse to promote innovation whilst optimising the operation of buildings for profit. In the market-driven landscape of co-working models, the former is usually a cover for the latter. The prevalent aesthetic of these spaces often leans on their industrial character: vast open-plan concrete floors, exposed pipework, an assortment of mismatched furniture, with the popular accessories of house plants and motivational signs and slogans promoting productivity in trendy fonts. This purposefully 'unfinished' aesthetic is meant to evoke the impression of unlimited entrepreneurial possibilities, again counting on individuals' malleability to be productive and creative in *any* condition. There is a myth that such flexible settings facilitate a higher degree of social networking and interactions among individuals, which can balance the pressure and anxiety of being constantly creative.

Yet, the less-discussed aspects of flexibility are labour conditions, precarious employment with low and sometimes non-existent wages, multiple jobs, and emotional stress,[5] which justifies and even drives the proliferation of precarious working conditions.

Within the creative industry's discourse, artists or independent cultural producers are framed as so-called *culturepreneurs*,[6] conflating creativity with the ability to dream up new products and services to bring to the market. Theories on the creative economy often merge cultural and economic values, understanding art and culture as a means for creating surplus value: creative entrepreneurialism. The approach to flexibility in these physical spaces, and the promise of networking, comes at the cost of the privatisation of creativity, resulting in either less space for more money, or the pushing out of types of production that are not as easily marketable or profitable.

Today many creative workspaces favour certain types of production – prioritising digital production (graphic design, animation, video editing) over physical making (carpentry, printmaking, ceramics) or performance (choreography, music production, theatre).[7] The latter types of production require secure space to keep tools and equipment, to leave unfinished work, or the space to move, make noise and rehearse. These types of production include noisy, messy, space-hungry practices that do not fit neatly into sanitised, desk-based co-working

1 Florida, R. (2002) *The Rise of the Creative Class.*

2 Bridges, E. (2017) "Flexible as freedom? The dynamics of creative industry work and the case study of the editor in publishing". *New Media & Society*, 20(4): 1303–19.

3 For example the use of culture in urban regeneration. See Evans, G. and Shaw, P. (2004) *The contribution of culture to regeneration in the UK: a review of evidence.* For more on this, and on the use of culture in city branding see Jensen, O. B. (2005) "Branding the contemporary city: urban branding, as regional growth agenda?". Plenary paper for Regional Studies Association Conference 'Regional Growth Agenda' (Aalborg University).

4 Pratt, A. C. (2008) "Creative cities: The cultural industries and the creative class". *Geografiska Annaler Series B-Human Geography*, 90B(2): 107–17; Schlesinger, P. (2017) "The creative economy: invention of a global orthodoxy". *Innovation: The European Journal of Social Science Research*, 30(1): 73–90.

5 Merkel, J. (2015) "Co-working in the city". *Ephemera*, 15(2): 121–39.

6 The term *culturepreneurs* describes the emergence of a new hybrid cultural and entrepreneurial agent in the context of the creative industries.

7 For more on these generic types see Bingham-Hall, J. and Kaasa, A. (2017) *Making Cultural Infrastructure: Can We Design the Conditions for Culture?*

Elahe Karimnia

environments. The space for digital production can be less specific, can happen anywhere and can be accessed at any time and by anyone. Such hypotheses have resulted in the proliferation of precarious working conditions masked by the promise of flexibility and creativity, which in reality means the users of these spaces compromise on many levels.

So what does flexibility mean to those producers whose practice sits at the margins of the creative industries and who don't benefit from this model? Dancers, musicians, painters and craftspeople have different spatial requirements, be it size, specific equipment, or visibility. Is flexibility always a form of precariousness?

I am particularly interested in examining these questions from the perspective of small-scale, independent cultural producers whose practices have limited commercial opportunities. By looking closely at a few individual cultural producers and their workspaces, I seek to uncover how flexibility manifests in the relationships between these individuals, the resources they need for their practice, and how their workspaces are designed and managed. To do so, I am drawing on the conversations I had with cultural producers while visiting their workspaces in railway arches (Elephant and Castle, London), reused market buildings (The Barras, Glasgow), and publicly funded *meanwhile*[8] projects (Belsunce, Marseille). The selected case studies offer specific operational models in terms of the finance, management and occupation of these spaces, which act as infrastructure for cultural production and illustrate the diversity of what we imagine as creative work in these cities.[9]

The Space, The Barras, Glasgow

The Space is based within a former furniture store, which was converted in 2015 into Scotland's first pay-what-you-decide community arts venue run by volunteers from the charity People Without Labels. It was awarded a public grant from Keep Scotland Beautiful to reuse the building and create a social hub for homeless people to bring them closer to art and culture. The building operation relies on crowdfunding and donations, as well as rent from workspaces and venues to hire, which are all diverted to its main social mission – to support the local community – leaving little to no margin for profit. The Barras is a historic neighbourhood currently undergoing a council-led process of regeneration to become a locus for arts and culture, with several new creative hubs opening in adapted derelict buildings over the last decade (such as The Pipe Factory, Barras Art and Design, Glasgow Collective and Many Studios).

Colours of the iron cage

On the ground floor of the four-storey building, behind a big metal garage door which opens onto the street, I meet Sue, a graduate art student and painter, in her workspace. While entering her studio from inside the building, I am immediately dazzled by an enormous metal cage built to fit the space. Paint dripping from hung objects has caused chaos on the floor, while cans of spray paint sit in harmony, ready for their next performance. Sue describes her interest in pushing the boundaries of what we consider painting by playing with 'chance, gravity, suspension and luck'. Access to this place has allowed her the freedom to build this cage and has helped her to make her dream world real, but it comes with its own sacrifices. For Sue, the studio is not just a space in which to make art, but is the artwork itself. As the paint drips onto the floor, creating experimental forms, these improvised actions become part of the artistic process. She shares images and videos of the space and the

---

8   *Meanwhile* is a term describing a space (like an empty shop unit), a building (like an empty department store) or a place (like an empty site awaiting redevelopment). The term describes how the space might be used temporarily while it is empty or awaiting a long-term use, perhaps yet to be decided.

9   The characters and incidents portrayed in this essay are real, yet their names are fictitious.

process of making work live on social media to reveal the incomplete nature of creative work. In Sue's studio, flexibility can be seen in the ability to accommodate the artist's desire to build *dreams*, which gain a permanent presence. She believes such support for individual makers is part of the historic character of the neighbourhood, 'the DIY culture of the Barras', in Sue's words. Despite having to make and maintain her own workspace, she expressed concern about whether she could find a similar situation elsewhere, with access to a street-opening studio within a fifteen-minute walk of the city centre- for £250 a month, a space where she can dream up experimental work uninterrupted.

Whilst Sue has a monthly rolling contract, she is unsure how long she can afford to keep her studio. She has negotiated her rent through an open dialogue with the Space's managers, who are themselves volunteers in the building with uncertain roles. Flexibility here is a cooperation between the cultural producers in the building and the management who support culture for its own inherent value, rather than as a vehicle for profit.

I leave Sue's studio and wait for the manager to give me access to the first floor. The entrance hall has a ceiling covered with white cloth and is full of colourful images and signs, a collage of different tastes, among which I spot one of Sue's paintings. Looking around, there is a piano, two guitars and a few drums on the floor in the other corner, next to ten to fifteen pots of small plants fixed to the wall. Behind the door opening to the entrance hall labelled 'VENUE' is the 200-standing/60-seated capacity music venue, a gallery, and the beach, a temporary resting space for homeless or vulnerable members of the Calton community. The ground floor allows for an unusual co-habitation of different members of the comm nity (artists, volunteers, musicians, visitors, the homeless), but

only the cultural producers renting space here get to access the studios upstairs. The Space is unusual copared to other creative workspaces in that it also includes rehearsal space for musicians, alongside a mix of painters, sculptors, craftspeople and designers.

'45 show' from the nutshell   Upstairs, the first floor is subdivided with plywood partitions into workspaces of assorted sizes. Next to the staircase, there is a six-square-metre room with glued panels of polystyrene insulation on the walls, which its occupants, podcasters Colin and Joe, affectionately call the 'nutshell'. Doubling as a recording studio, Colin and Joe's goal is to reach out to undiscovered artists in the music scene to give them a chance to showcase their voices in their weekly podcasts, released every Saturday evening at six. Part of the attraction for them of being based in the Space is that the managers facilitate access to the music venue on the ground floor for their live recording of performances when the venue is not in use. In return, as Colin describes, they offered to create podcasts featuring musicians who use the Space's rehearsal rooms or the bands who occasionally have shows at the Space's music venue on the ground floor.

The timeline written on a little whiteboard on the wall showcases their workload that, as Joe explains, changes on a project-by-project basis, which allows them to adjust their schedule to work during less noisy times in the building, like weekends, and Mondays when the drummers who have a studio below are in. Flexibility is present not only in the physical rearrangement of the space but also in the manager's openness and cooperation, which enables the use of different spatial and social resources in the building.

    Elahe Karimnia

Boxed-in   On the next floor above Colin and Joe, Mona, a product designer who recently moved to Glasgow, has her studio. She is the only one working on this cold day. Her space is one of the eight units on the second floor; it is east-facing and smaller than the units with windows opening onto Bain Street. The space is full of different objects, and it is difficult to separate the artist's work from personal items: clothes, blankets left on chairs, photos pinned on the walls, unfinished paintings on the tripod in the middle of the room, brushes, portable radiators, water boilers, sculptures in the making, books, plants, and sketches.

Mona has personalised her space with a built structure on top of dividing wooden panels, covering her unit with transparent plastic sheets all the way to the ceiling. Mona told me that she had thought, 'I can either complain about how cold it is and pay a lot more money, or I can box myself in.' To cope, she has had to build an infrastructure within an existing infrastructure (the building). Mona has used her own time and labour to make these adaptations to make the space more environmentally comfortable, a compromise she is willing to make in order to save money on rent, which on that floor is £9 per square foot. Mona adjusts her practice to the size of this unit and compromises her

dream of making 'bigger, wilder things' in order to have the opportunity to leave unfinished work without having to store everything or sell it as quickly. But the size of the unit is not the only constraint on her work. Mona uses a furnace to melt aluminium cans and recast them into sculptural forms and figures. This process needs fresh air and cannot be done inside. Having no open-air workspace, she has to carry everything to the car park next to the building to make her work.

Robert Dashwood Way, Elephant and Castle, London   Robert Dashwood Way is a stretch of twenty-three Victorian railway arches, according to the information presented by Network Rail on the billboard at a corner of the street. The arches accommodate eighteen businesses, ranging from light industrial trade to car mechanics and auto repair, from textile and fashion production to storage for technical equipment and theatrical props. The railway arches were state-owned by Network Rail until their sale in 2019 to equity company Telereal Trillium and Blackstone Property Partners, and they are now managed privately by the Arch Company. Unlike the northern continuation of railway arches, which have been recently transformed into creative co-working spaces, Robert Dashwood Way has remained untouched. The businesses inside are mostly invisible, running behind the closed shutters, unlike the balconies and windows of the newly-built residentials on both sides, facing the road.

The backstage   A white van is unloaded on the street at dusk. Metal boxes are moved carefully on a trolley and pushed into one of the arches, the only one with open shutters. Ali and his business partner John run an audiovisual hire company which supplies major cultural venues and events in London's zone one, such as Borough Market and the Victoria and Albert Museum. The noise of passing trains resonates in Ali's workspace, where he is carefully guiding two men moving an LED Plasma screen to the back of the arch between huge boxes stacked on top of each other. Their business, London Audiovisual, serves as infrastructure for other cultural practices and supplies them with speakers, amplifiers, cables and stands. Rolling the shutters down, Ali shouts at the van driver, who is about to leave: 'Tomorrow! Six o'clock sharp! The conference is in the Waldorf Hilton.' He then turns to me and says, 'we are open whenever we need to be'.

For Ali, the central location is paramount in order to access their client base, some of which are London's major cultural institutions. Due to the extreme shortage of commercial premises suitable for light industrial practices or storage in central London, they chose to adapt their working model to suit the arches' less-than-ideal working conditions. Ali has made many alterations to the arches, such as adding shelves to the walls and adding a mezzanine in the back of the space, as well as expanding their business across several arches. Ali tells me, 'We've probably changed the layout eight times in the eight years we've been here'. They are willing to compromise on the environmental and material conditions of the arches, such as a lack of heating, Wi-Fi, natural light, the curved ceiling, which is not practical for vertical stacking, and the added labour of moving equipment between different lots. The noise of passing trains does not affect the work they do, moving, fixing and testing audiovisual equipment; in fact, it makes the railway arches a refuge for noisier, messier practices such as performance, light industrial making and music production that would otherwise struggle to find space within open-plan co-working models. The conflicts that have created issues for Ali's company are those with the residential neighbours living in developments that have sprung up around Robert Dashwood Way in the last decade. Residents complain about the noise the company makes while loading their vans with equipment early in the morning or closing the noisy metal shutters at night.

The main incentive for Ali in making these compromises has been the long-term leases offered by the previous landlord, Network Rail. Their benign neglect in managing these spaces,[10] which for many years were considered as left-over subsidiary spaces to the railway above, can be adapted without a planning application due to their square footage of less than five hundred square feet. Although the tenants of these arches have the freedom to adapt their space, extra square footage added to the premises is factored into the council charges.

The combination of adaptability, affordability and long-term lease that Network Rail has provided as a landlord has given these businesses the stability they require to survive and simultaneously support cultural production in central London. However, this is subject to change in the future, as the ownership of railway arches has been transferred to the private sector.

Invisible fashion A few arches down the road, Katie runs her small business as a fashion designer behind the almost always closed roller shutter. From 2D illustration, through sample making to production, all of Katie's work is done in this space. Her arch was previously used as storage for her family's Chinese restaurant until Katie got a government grant to start her own fashion and textile business. Now that her parents are retired, she takes care of both her own business and her family's restaurant, which has been a neighbourhood institution for more than sixteen years. Working early mornings, Katie starts at six o'clock to receive all the ingredients for traditional Cantonese cuisine, and then before lunch, she walks five minutes back to her studio to check the designers' progress and finish her own work. 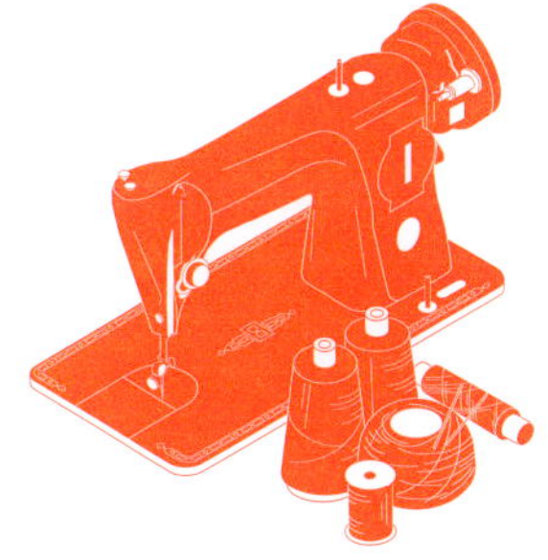 She returns to the restaurant late at night to take care of cleaning and other duties. Katie acknowledges the convenience of having two businesses next to each other, allowing her the flexibility to bounce between her fashion business and the family business.

Katie, like Ali, mentions the advantage of the arches' adaptability and affordability, allowing her to refurbish the space, which required a lot of labour, as it was rented as an empty shell. Katie's space is completely hidden by a blank roller shutter, and she tells me that having no public interface is an advantage. 'I want the least daily

10   For many years the railway arches have been considered by-product subsidiary spaces of the train network, undesirable spaces for developers to invest in, which has protected them until now. "Landlord Network Rail has been benignly neglecting them partly due to their sheer number, partly due to their supporting role to the railway". Kostourou, F., Chua, C., and Karimnia, E. (2019), p. 63.

     Elahe Karimnia

interruptions,' she says. She added a mezzanine in the back of the arch to provide space for sewing machines, pattern-cutting tables, steaming equipment, rolls of fabric and clothing rails. The space is divided between a fashion studio, where Katie works with two designers cutting patterns, and storage for her family's restaurant. With only six years left on Katie's lease, the Arch Company has already warned her that, due to the ongoing regeneration in the area, there is a possibility of a rent increase.

Located a stone's throw from Saint-Charles (Marseille's main railway station) and Porte d'Aix (Marseille's Arc de Triomphe), Coco Velten is a project that offers fifty-five affordable workshops/offices (€10 per square metre), eighty spaces of emergency housing for homeless families, a canteen as a meeting point, a rooftop terrace as an experimental collaboration, and venues for a public programme. Situated within the dense and deprived neighbourhood of Belsunce, Coco Velten is a mixed-use, hybrid space connecting culture and public life. It was envisioned as a catalyst for transforming the neighbourhood by creating solidarity between local stakeholders to collaborate and make experimental work together. Hidden in a gated courtyard, Coco

Velten was initiated through a meanwhile occupancy (2019 – 2021) of an empty late nineteenth-century building. Owned and fully funded by the state, it represents a public-private hybridity through which a third party manages cultural institutions to initiate and develop innovative solutions to complex urban issues. It is co-organised by partners Yes We Camp (responsible for the building and public programmes), Plateau Urbain (responsible for actors and their employment) and Groupe SOS (responsible for emergency housing). Due to limited funding and the temporary nature of the project, Yes We Camp prioritised basic refurbishments and light touches such as new signage, paint and posters to create safe working and living spaces for occupants. No significant improvements were made to the workspaces, but a canteen, rooftop terrace and other public venues within the building were designed to generate income for the project. From the outdoor space of the canteen where I stand, I can see children running around the courtyard of the îlot Velten, playing on the grass and around the basketball field. A few of them run in and out of the canteen freely, and it seems the staff members know them well.

Leyla is a fabric designer who rents a studio in Coco Velten, where she and her design collective met during an interdisciplinary exchange programme. Her practice is focused on reducing waste, rehabilitation, and reuse, and she chose to work at Coco Velten because she shares similar social values and an environmental commitment consistent with the project's mission. Leyla shows me her work, unfoling patterns and ornaments made of recycled materials collected from the neighbourhood in collaboration with

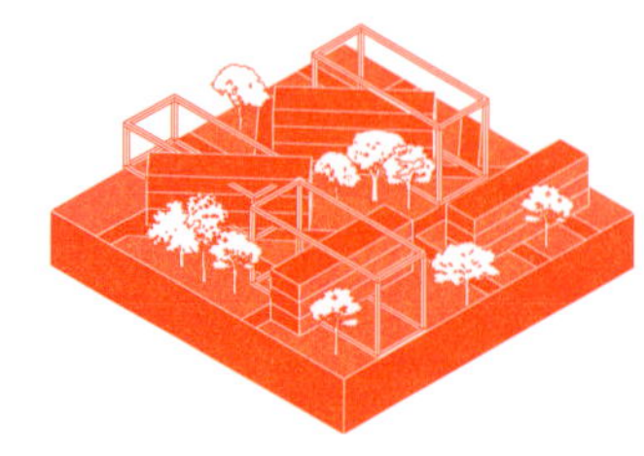

members of the local community. Leyla points at the colourful tiles hung in one corner of her studio, which were made in a workshop she ran for kids to uncover Belsunce's social, spatial and material history through collecting found objects.

The flexibility in the social and cultural use of the building manifests at Coco Velten on different scales. On the one hand, the project's public performance at the level of hosting events, such as the Manifesta Biennale, provides many opportunities for cultural creatives to meet; the same can be said for the events staged at the building and the canteen, which according to Leyla, have expanded their professional network and initiated collaborations. On the other hand, its physical and social openness to the neighbourhood can result in lost visitors and children playing in the corridors, which can be a distraction for those renting workspace here. The workspace Leyla and her colleagues share at Coco Velten is small and more suited to desk-based work, and as she explains, there is not enough space for running workshops, building prototypes, storing materials, and meeting clients. Now that they have two separate offices, they can focus better on work, but Leyla thinks it sometimes hinders the sharing of information.

Leyla appreciates the organisers' ethics, openness, and willingness to run the building as a democratic platform for different actors interested in civic projects. While most of the practices that rent space within Coco Velten could operate within a co-working space, this model is elevated by being a social enterprise. Managing such a social enterprise requires day-to-day experimentation in order to avoid commercial activities outweighing social and cultural objectives or staff burnouts.

Flexibility in cultural production As explored in these workspaces, flexibility is not a mission or goal; it is just an integral and inevitable part of small-scale and independent cultural production that enables it to survive austerity and to resist the marketisation of creative industries. The flexibility that these (co)working spaces offer is the possibility to experiment, to adapt the space and to care about values other than profitability. Flexibility manifests itself in these individuals' improvised tactics and adjustments, borne out of creativity, constraints, or care, or perhaps all three at once.

The Space – Flexibility as experimentation:
Compromise, in relation to the lack of suitable environmental and spatial conditions, has meant that cultural producers in the Space have had to build their own infrastructures. Whilst this condition (lack of funding and material comfort) should not be romanticised, it has given the people working there more freedom for experimentation. This experimentation was observed in each individual's practices and the way it has shaped the work they produce, but also in the different ways tenants exchanged skills and resources in the building.

Robert Dashwood Way – Flexibility as adaptation:
Flexibility here has been defined by compromising ideal or adequate space for affordability, location, and opportunity for reconfiguration. The railway arches are less than ideal in terms of noise, light, form, or ventilation, but they have offered unlimited possibilities for reconfiguration, and their long-term leases created affordable, stable workspaces while under the ownership of Network Rail. The invisibility of these spaces supports practices that do not benefit from public display or footfall, and need privacy in order to produce their work. Flexibility in spatial adaptation is possible when there is a long-term lease or enough stability for the producer, no matter how uncertain their practice gets.

Coco Velten – Flexibility as inclusiveness:
Flexibility here has been defined by a social and economic model through which the space is granted under the condition of inclusivity and with care for social and environmental values. Renting space at Coco Velten is

contingent on being prepared to interact and collaborate with the buildings surrounding the community, as part of its commitment to the cultural regeneration of the area. The cultural producers renting space here need to be aligned with the ethics and mission of the building for this model to work.

Each of the cultural producers interviewed has made some kind of compromise in terms of their space and its unfinished infrastructure. Flexibility is the compatibility between constraints of space (its form, material, regulations), an individual's creativity and social support. The arguments unfolded in this essay provide multiple different readings of what flexibility is and can be, beyond a buzzword linked to co-working spaces. The photogenic spaces of the co-working model only fulfil the needs of a very specific type of cultural producer and are more akin to precarity. Melting materials, spraying objects, making sculptures, recording podcasts, storing expensive and bulky audiovisual equipment, sewing clothes, or initiating community projects can't happen in these types of spaces. However, it is these practices, and the voices and stories behind this work, that are vital for feeding the cultural life of our cities.

Invisible Neighbourhoods

Fani Kostourou

1   See, for example, The Student Room [thestudentroom.co.uk/showthread. php?t=3297279] and Quora forums [quora .com/Whats-it-like-to-live-in-Elephant -and-Castle]; GoodMigrations city guide [goodmigrations.com/city-guides /london/elephant-and-castle]; Tripsget travel blog [https://tripsget.com/living-in -elephant-and-castle-london-is-elephant -and-castle-dangerous/]; Home Made Blog (2022) [blog.home-made.com/living-in -elephant-and-castle/]; Yopa estate agent [yopa.co.uk/homeowners-hub/whats-it -like-to-live-in-elephant-and-castle/]; and *Evening Standard* newspaper [standard .co.uk/homesandproperty/where-to-live /living-in-elephant-castle-area-guide -to-homes-schools-and-transport -links-a135826.html].

2   In a *Time Out* readers' poll in 2005. [https://www.london-se1.co.uk/news /view/1496].

3   After WWII and during the 1960s, the area got earmarked for redevelopment as part of a slum clearance initiative. A new urban plan was developed by the city and masterminded by Erno Goldfinger that included high-rise housing blocks like the Heygate Estate, university complexes like UAL's London College of Communication, and the first covered shopping centre in Europe. Read more: Allies and Morrison (2016), *Elephant and Castle Town Centre: Design And Access Statement.*

4   Collins, M. (2001) "The Elephant's grave yard", The Guardian [theguardian .com/theobserver/2001/dec/23/life1 .lifemagazine1].

5   According to the 2011 Census, about eight thousand Latin Americans live in Southwark, representing just under three per cent of the borough's population and eight per cent of the residents who were born outside of the UK. See more: Berg, M.L. (2019) "Super-diversity, austerity, and the production of precarity: Latin Americans in London". *Critical Social Policy*, 39(2): 184–204; and Krausova, A. (2016) "Latin Americans in Southwark: A Census Analysis Report". Centre on Migration, Policy and Society.

6   For a detailed account of the struggles between Southwark Council, Delancey, traders and action groups, over the neglect to relocate traders post-development, see: Latin Elephant (2020) "Elephant and Castle redevelopment: Displaced traders with no relocation" [latinelephant.org /displaced-traders-with-no-relocation/] and Petit Elephant and Peluffo, S. (2019) Elephant and Castle [latinelephant.org /map/#headline].

I walk up the steps of the Elephant and Castle tube station and onto the streets of a neighbourhood I have read a lot about since I decided to move to the British capital. As an urban researcher investigating where and how culture happens in the city, I had thought of the neighbourhood as a major road junction, unloved by Londoners despite being well connected to other parts of the city. I discovered a few blogs profiling it as an unsafe place to be out and about at night due to gangs operating in the area, while other websites mentioned its poor street planning, intricate web of underpasses, and rundown buildings that have never received necessary attention.[1] The film *Harry Brown* (2009) was shot in and around the Heygate Estate, a modernist council estate completed in 1974 which was demolished between 2011 and 2014. Using the estate as a backdrop for stories of youth crime, the film contributed to the image of the neighbourhood as a violent place. However, the area appears to be undergoing a process of transformation, which, in the minds of its planners, architects and developers, promises to give it a new lease of life.

As I exit the station, I see a mix of pre-war buildings, council estates, and high-rises. A traffic-dominated roundabout unfolds before my eyes, and the scale of the place contrasts with the narrow Parisian streets of La Goutte d'Or neighbourhood, which has been the focus of my research so far.

Passing by the showroom of a newly finished housing block, I pick up a brochure from an Australian developer featuring photoshopped birds-eye-view renders of the new redevelopment of the neighbourhood that surrounds me. It lists all the benefits of the plan: new employment opportunities, shops, restaurants, leisure and retail spaces, offices, new houses, and a new building for the London College of Communication. Its imagery and language come across as utopian and overly optimistic as if there is a targeted effort to convince the readers of the project. A whole new town centre will be built where I now see a few bulldozers tearing down the Elephant and Castle Shopping Centre. Voted London's ugliest building,[2] I always imagined it as an unloved landmark, reminiscent of the last major masterplan of the area.[3] Whilst some described it as ugly and grotesque, a graveyard and an eyesore, others, particularly the Latin American community (Colombians, Ecuadorians, Peruvians, Bolivians and Chileans), have revitalised it by opening shops, travel agents, bureaux de change, cafés, and stalls.[4] In the years before its demolition, the shopping centre was the most vibrant it had been, but what I now see left behind are colourful protest banners hanging from the railing of its ruined balcony:

LOVE THE ELEPHANT – HATE GENTRIFICATION
THE LONDON LATINXS PROTECT OUR BARRIOS
ELEPHANT ALWAYS IN OUR HEART
DEMOLISH DELANCEY
STOP THE ELEPHANT DEVELOPMENT

A report by Latin Elephant, a campaign group supporting the local migrant communities, highlighted the dispersal of around a hundred independent traders. Elephant and Castle was, and still is, one of the two areas in London closely associated with Latin American and other diasporic populations.[5] There used to be retailers from Brazil, Colombia, Nigeria, Ghana, Afghanistan, India and other countries. They operated small-scale businesses including restaurants, cafés, jewellery making, clothing production, computer repairs, homeware, accessories, shipping, travel and money transfer services, and hairdressers. The new developer, Delancey, had promised to relocate them to affordable retail units in nearby locations.[6] Some merchants had been in the market for more than twenty years, and although they did the paperwork, made calls, went to the council, the business and relocation advisor's office, and countless other meetings, they were not offered a place for trading in the new development. Amongst them were even a few who were promised help should they remain at the

　　　　Fani Kostourou

building during the negotiations and who continued to pay rent but were not given space in the new development.

There is a striking difference between how local traders were treated during the regeneration of Elephant and Castle compared to what happened in La Goutte d'Or neighbourhood in Paris. It was six years ago when the mayor of the eighteenth arrondissement, to which,

La Goutte d'Or belongs, partnered with local artisans and textile shop owners to set up a local business centre around fashion and design in order to bring together professionals operating in the industry and organise the provision of their services.[7] The goal was for both the council and the designers, tailors and traders to boost local economic activity, employment and entrepreneurship. Unlike the dispersion policy of Elephant and Castle's redevelopment, in La Goutte d'Or there has been a shared interest to value, keep, and empower – through formalisation – the various manufacturing activities that happen at the district level. The council saw the benefit of working with the existing potential of the area, either by refurbishing abandoned premises or joining forces with the local migrant communities from North and sub-Saharan Africa who immigrated to the area from the early twentieth century and throughout the 1950s.[8]

In La Goutte d'Or, there are currently many migrant couturiers, fashion designers, grocers, bakers, halal butchers, hairdressers, merchants of African clothes, textiles and haberdashery, as well as young creatives who work in the arts and crafts. Most of them are organised around the street of Myrha (rue Myrha). Its pavements are so narrow that you cannot cross them. People pull their shopping carts right in the middle of the road, dodging cyclists. On a good day, from west to east and in its parallel and perpendicular streets, I would watch informal street stalls selling corn whilst listening to Afrobeats coming from a couple of label stores. I would get a stock of fresh free-range eggs from the local farm – the only farm inside Paris that sells live poultry – enjoy the colourful fabrics behind the windows of small African boutiques, and spend time rummaging through art books at the little

bookstore/craft workshop space. At lunchtime, I would pass outside the *Institut des Cultures d'Islam* (Institute of Islamic Culture) and the nearby cafés and restaurants to smell the *thieboudienne* with *mafé* or *yassa*, a famous Senegalese recipe. At the centre of this hive of activity is *la couture*, particularly the African fashion community of designers, tailors, textile fabricators and pattern cutters. Through the establishment of the local business centre, the quarter has redefined its basis for economic development. It has achieved greater visibility from the outside, building up a dedicated clientele and investing in the infrastructure that supports the migrant culture of its local community.

But it was not always like this. Similarly to Elephant and Castle, La Goutte d'Or did not have a good reputation.[9] In the nineteenth century, Émile Zola described the neighbourhood as a claustrophobic, working-class suburb plagued by misery, alcoholism, violence and prostitution.[10] During the 1990s, rue Myrha was nicknamed 'death row', the most dangerous street in Paris, and one of the most infamous crack cocaine hotspots in the city. There were a lot of drugs, squats, and buildings in ruins, but over the last few years, the area has been transformed. Organic canteens, vegan restaurants,

7   In 2016, there were approximately 150 designers in the area. See Guinebault, M. (2016) "Fabrique de La Goutte d'Or: une coopérative textile Made in Paris", Fashion Network [/fr.fashionnetwork .com/news/Fabrique-de-la-goutte-d -or-une-cooperative-textile-made-in -paris,679973.html].

8   The big immigration wave took place in the 1950s to access work in the automobile industry. By the end of the decade La Goutte-d'Or was so heavily populated with Algerians that it became the headquarters of the National Liberation Front during the Algerian war. See Vallois, T. (1999) "Around and About Paris, The 13th-20th arrondissements", *Paris Voice* [parisvoice.com/goutte-dorafrica-in-paris/].

9   La Goutte d'Or was the first Parisian district to become a *Zone de Securité Prioritaire* (priority safety zone) in 2012, then a *Quartier de Renconquête Républiquaine* (republican reconquest district) in 2019. For more on the reinforced police presence these policies introduced, the symbolic anti-immigration invocation of Muslims praying in the street by the Far Right, who claimed the area was a no-go zone, as well as the safety incidents in the area related to drug use, see Musca, H. (2020) "Rue Myrha, la grande transformation d'un faubourg malfamé de Paris", *Le Figaro* [lefigaro.fr /actualite-france/rue-myrha-la-grande -transformation-d-un-faubourg-malfame -de-paris-20201212].

10   Zola says that rue Myrha, in the book *Rue de La Goutte d'Or*, 'didn't exactly smell of roses!' Zola, É. (1877) *The Assommoir*. Reprint 2021. Translated by Brian Nelson, p. 247.

Invisible Neighbourhoods

high fashion brands made of African textiles and ultra-hip stores have sprung up, and several social housing units, two student residencies as well as a music factory have been built on former wastelands or squats. It all started with an effort from the municipality to acquire local premises, rebuild them gradually over time, respecting the scale and size of existing units, and rent them affordably to different small businesses, ensuring diversity in their economic activities. Although the rent has almost doubled in five years, many of the families that used to live there can still afford to cover it, for it remains well below the city average.[11] Alongside older residents, newcomers have settled down in the quarter. There is a much more *bobo* (bourgeois and bohemian) population living here now, made up of young people who either have good positions in companies or are artists. This demographic wants to live in Paris, not necessarily in the centre of it, but wants to experience 'real' neighbourhood life. Of course, problems still exist in the area – such as informal economic transactions, violence, and crime, especially a few meters down on Panama Street (rue de Panama), – but at least there has been an effort to avoid repeating the mistakes of the past redevelopment that took place in southern La Goutte d'Or in the 1960s and 1970s.[12] These past efforts erased most of the historic fabric of the area by erecting mass concrete housing blocks, whose design cut them off from the street and its everyday life.

As I continue walking, I see the large-lettered advertisement on the hoarding of Elephant and Castle Shopping Centre, which brings me back into the present moment. All this time, I was walking along the perimeter of the demolition site. Motivational verbs of promises like CREATE, INSPIRE, DISCOVER, and EXPLORE mingle with less formal tagging by street artists: I LOVE THIS, HOW'D U GET SO GOOD? Above and behind the black metal panels, the red-and-white sign of the Bingo Club, subtitled 'The London Palace', is the only souvenir of what used to be a well-frequented social and leisure hub that, just like the rest of the covered market, has been emptied of life due to the recent planning decisions.

My thoughts are disrupted as I am distracted by the aroma of freshly baked pastries from the other side of the street. I follow my nose and walk parallel to the tracks in front of the railway arches. The first stretch of arches on Elephant Road elaborate shop fronts with aluminium frames and colourful signage. Arch 7 is open, and I catch a glimpse of a multitude of activities inside – a restaurant and café, money transfer, ladies' fashion, international shipping, real-estate agencies, and hairdressers. Walking further down, I pass under the railway tracks and find myself on Maldonado Walk, a small alleyway which has recently been renamed after an Ecuadorian scientist. I feel squeezed between the brick walls of the arches and Strata Tower, a forty-three-storey residential building, which was also – ironically – voted the ugliest building in the UK two years after it was built and seven years after the shopping centre facing it won the same title. The bespoke design of the tower, the glass façade and wind turbines, come in contrast to the completely DIY appearance of the arches on the opposite side. The door and windows of Arch 6 are open, and four advertisements animate the façade. As I enter, I am amazed by the concentration of people and activities in such a tiny space. People move and work between partitions, on mezzanine floors above or behind counters and curtains. At the back, there is a Colombian café. They are taking *Almojábanas* out of the oven, a delectable round concoction made of cornmeal, butter, and mozzarella. I notice that the café shares the ground floor with seven other micro-businesses, while a beauty, hair-dressing and tattoo salon occupies the mezzanine. I am told that the lady who runs it is Colombian and that the majority of her clients, like those of the café, are

11 According to the Chambre des Notaires de Paris, in August 2020 the price per square meter in rue Myrha was €8,760 and the average price per sqm in Paris was €10,750. [paris.notaires.fr /ruemyrha2005]

12 Ibid.

13 The most commonly used main language besides English in Elephant and Castle is Spanish (2,400 residents), representing 12% of all residents who reported a main spoken language other than English and 2.7% of the total population of the area. Many of those residents are likely from Latin America. See Krausova, A. (2018) "Elephant and Castle: Mapping (Super-)Diversity in the 2011 UK Census". Centre on Migration, Policy and Society, 18–142: 1–28.

Fani Kostourou

Latin. I can hear her chatting with clients in Spanish while fixing their hair and nails.[13] With an *Almojábanas* in hand, I start walking again and pass by more stretches of railway arches. The next row, Spare Street, looks recently repaved, and the arched walls feature fully glazed façade with trendy graphic-designed lettering. A co-working company manages the space and provides commercial units to artists and small businesses. An architecture firm occupies the front of the arch and represents the way the space communicates itself to the public. At the end of Spare Street, the stretch of the next arches is five times as long but gated at each end.

The repetition of the same arched pattern now becomes monotonous, as most of the arches have their roller shutters down. There is nothing to observe, and the complete absence of windows and signs from the street makes me wonder what is hiding behind the closed shutters. I see a man moving some equipment and immediately approach him to ask what is going on within. He tells me he runs an audiovisual supply

company that provides venues with big projections, plasma screens, LED lighting and audio equipment. His clients are mainly hotels, museums and offices in central London. He likes the area because it is central. The man also talks to me about his neighbours. Next door to him, there is a theatre company that supplies staging weights and props, whilst further down the road there is a fashion design studio run by a Chinese tailor. While these types of businesses need to be easily accessible, they do not need to be visible from the outside, as they benefit from operating in the background of other activities or spaces. They are used for light manufacturing, supplier-oriented services, or storage, which do not rely on the footfall of passers-by and therefore do not require windows, signs, or other forms of display. Most of the time, they don't need to advertise on-site, for this can be done simply through word of mouth or social media. In contrast, some businesses seek to attract consumers and become destinations, and can thus benefit more from a public-facing marketing strategy. This is true for Spare Street and Maldonado Walk, both of which have tried to open up their interface towards the street. The first has done so formally, through the architect's design and installation of a fully-glazed façade. In the second case, the traders have built these interfaces themselves, perforating them using cheap construction materials, like steel frames, breeze blocks, and prefab windows, and populating them with colourful signs and papers. They have also tried to gain visibility by branding this cluster of activities as the 'Latin Quarter', using the title to campaign for the rights of all migrant-owned businesses in the neighbourhood and create a network of solidarity among them.

All three types of activities (invisible, visible by design, visible through solidarity) are accommodated in the same typology, which is by default a by-product of another activity and its physical infrastructure (railway). This ensures another level of invisibility and anonymity, which can be useful if, for example, a business offers community-led integration advice services for migrants, like the Colombian café, or looks to keep their valuable premises and products secure, as in the case of the audio supply company. The spatial typology of the railway arch, owned by the public body of Network Rail, has had, until now, the capacity to combine multiple programmes, maximising the potential of a functional space whilst keeping it outside the prime real estate market, thus preventing rents from rising steeply as part of the regeneration process. In this sense, invisibility at some level can be an important asset because it can protect the infrastructures of certain activities, meaning the networks of people, information, processes and physical structures that underlie them and ensure their longevity.

These infrastructures support activities of culture whilst operating in the background of everyday life in cities and neighbourhoods. They include – besides buildings and utilities – everything from stories to routines, recipes, technologies, signs, human labour, ownership models and social networks, as well as the traces of all those things that existed before them. Just like any other kind of infrastructure – highways, pipes, cables, laws, and land divisions, to name a few – they order and shape most of the spaces we see, feel, experience, or interact with. They are not hidden, just invisible and sometimes intangible, like council policies and community protests. Nonetheless, they organise the functioning of an entire neighbourhood or city and, in the case of infrastructures for cultural activities, shape the identity of that place.

Often, infrastructures are invisible because there are deliberate human actions undertaken to hide them behind hoarding, inactive frontages, planning documents, or political decisions. Sometimes, they become invisible over time, as they slowly start to go unnoticed and disappear from people's awareness and consciousness.[14] Then, it takes a major event in the life of a neighbourhood – like the approval of the redevelopment of Elephant and Castle and the demolition of its shopping centre – to shift the focus beyond what meets the public eye. What such an event does at the scale of the neighbourhood is to reveal the disconnect between what the authorities, contractors and planners promise, what the people need and desire, and what the urban space is actually doing. In other words, it exposes the misalignment between the rhetoric adopted by key developers and the council and the reality on the ground voiced by protesters and the residents and traders of the Latin American and diasporic communities. Architectural theorist Keller Easterling claims that such misalignment of urban narratives lends an urban space an 'accidental, and covert disposition', and through this tool of disposition, infrastructures become visible, gain agency and the ability to instigate change and determine the present and future of urban spaces and the communities that inhabit them.[15]

I translate *disposition* into the latent potential of a neighbourhood to serve a social, cultural, economic, and political role within the context of a city.[16] The current disposition of Elephant and Castle results from all of its activities, as much as its role as an important transport node centrally located within a metropolitan city. On the one hand, this demonstrates a dynamic mix of diverse socio-economic groups and practices, historical traces, and built forms, and on the other hand, it fosters solidarity among diasporic populations and the light industrial and supply businesses that have found refuge within the railway arches.[17] While the former is easily visible, felt, and understood by the majority of people, the latter is not. A decision to redevelop the area based solely on its visible infrastructures carries the risk of irreversibly changing its current disposition, forever terminating its social and cultural role as activities and communities will be displaced and replaced by other profit-driven ones that are more favourable to the capitalist market. It might have made more sense, instead, to regenerate Elephant and Castle (and adjust its disposition) by maximising its potential, respecting and protecting the invisibility of some of its activities, spaces, and infrastructures, whilst taking advantage of the larger networks and urban systems that these connect to. This way, the transformation would extend the life of its social and cultural resources, strengthen its unique role within the city and contribute to the longer-term sustainability of the neighbourhood.

When the city authorities decided to redevelop La Goutte d'Or, they did so by investing in its invisible infrastructure.

14   Paul N. Edwards argues that for the majority of people, infrastructure becomes embedded in the habits and skills of individuals through a process of 'infrastructuration', that is a familiarisation process with what constantly works around us as long as they work well and stay the same. See Edwards, P.N. (2017) "The Mechanics of Invisibility: On Habit and routine as Elements of Infrastructure" in I. Ruby and A. Ruby (eds.), *Infrastructure Space*, pp. 327–36, p. 330.

15   Easterling, K. (2016) *Extrastatecraft*, p. 73.

16   Keller Easterling defines disposition as the 'latent potential or tendency that is present even in the absence of an event', its propensity within a context or in an arrangement. For more, see ibid., p. 72, p. 83.

17   Elephant and Castle is home to the largest and oldest Latin American business cluster in London with 130 businesses. The socio-economic value of the neighbourhood is addressed extensively in King, J. et al (2018) "Socio-economic value at the Elephant and Castle" [http://eprints.lse.ac.uk/90160/1/Hall__socio-economic-value.pdf].

They chose to safeguard what was happening in the background to increase the chances of local activities growing and flourishing in the future. Not only could the neighbourhood represent North and sub-Saharan African culture and craftsmanship, but it could also turn into a melting pot of several cultures. The municipality took advantage of the spatial clustering of textile and fashion design creatives and the sense of solidarity among the African community. They also saw the potential of refurbishing properties and offering small affordable units to local independent producers and traders.

In turn, these independent producers were invited to sit at the same table as the decision makers, communicate their objectives publicly and band together to form two legal entities: the *Association des Professionnels de la Mode et du Design de La Goutte d'Or* (Association of Fashion and Design Professionals of La Goutte d'Or) and the artisan cooperative *La Fabrique de La Goutte d'Or* (The Factory of La Goutte d'Or).[18] Cur-

rently, the former assembles local professionals that operate in the textiles, fashion, and design sector, and the latter serves as a pool of local textile-related services. The two formats complement each other. The association allows individuals to gain legal and economic status, access public funding and deal with marketing and public relations, while the cooperative organises the production of clothes behind the scenes and develops and disseminates knowledge. The first is relatively visible, both physically and virtually, but the second is not. Yet both are created infrastructures that tap into existing networks and actively shape the potential and role of the neighbourhood.

The anonymity that these infrastructures offer to individual businesses allows them to bypass bureaucracies and formal legal protocols in order to be more agile, taking advantage of their own invisibility within an international system that mediates goods and media. For instance, there are tailors in La Goutte d'Or that have clients in Brussels or Switzerland who come regularly there because they have family in Paris. Through my research I met designers who collaborate with fabric wholesalers outside of Paris, from Bobigny, Aubervilliers, Saint-Denis or Saclay. Some boutiques use fabrics that are produced in Mali or Senegal, and others work with wax printing factories in Cote d'Ivoire. Often, large-volume orders are produced in Tunisia and transferred to Paris. These commercial transactions and relations would not have been so easily established had a state-funded association based in France initiated them.

The association and the cooperative have 'spatially rewired' the neighbourhood at a local scale through a 'topology' of small shops and ateliers, a collaboration that remodels flows of activities, information, and routines.[19] In addition, the individuals behind or outside the association and the cooperative have activated remote sites in the larger urban, national, and international landscape. As a result, this has widened the networks and established new geo-political, social, and ecological relations beyond the administrative boundaries of the neighbourhood, affecting its local conditions and disposition.

Lost in thoughts about La Goutte d'Or, I reach the Victorian tenement buildings of Pullens Yards, a live-work scheme occupied by artists and built in the 1860s, a few blocks west of the railway arches. On the wall at the entrance of the estate, I read that there is a tenant and residents' association to manage the place, safeguard the rents and organise biannual open studios. Southwark council owns the yards and acts as their landlord, while the Residents Association manages them and negotiates rent. The complicated power dynamics

18   For more on this, see the Les Gouttes d'Or de la mode et du design website [www.madeingouttedor.paris].

19   Keller Easterling talks about spatial wiring and topology as an active form in infrastructure space that can help mark its disposition. See: Easterling, K. (2016) *Extrastatecraft*, p. 76–78.

between authorities and individuals or associations, whether tenants or artisans, are everywhere the same.

La Goutte d'Or association and cooperative are the outcomes of the convergence of a top-down and a bottom-up initiative to redevelop a struggling, centrally located, immigration-linked neighbourhood. The neighbourhood is in the process of negotiating its potential whilst activating its invisible infrastructures of migrant economies, community, and culture at the urban as well as international level. This model prioritises the diversification of the neighbourhood, the protection of the socio-economic value of small-scale local production and the legitimisation of smaller migrant infrastructures in urban space. Although it is still a work in progress, it is a formula that creates visible infrastructures for invisible neighbourhoods. If the model and formula prove successful, could they be applied to other neighbourhoods that face similar problems? Could they benefit other cities like London?

As I walk back to the tube station, I am full of new images, sounds, smells, colours, and textures, registered in my body. I realise it takes an effort to see beyond the first impression of a neighbourhood, to read beyond what is clearly visible and understand the latent potential of its infrastructures. Elephant and Castle is certainly an example of a neighbourhood whose disposition has changed multiple times through the years and will once again change as a result of the ongoing regeneration plan. The brochure only visualises part of its disposition, narratives scripted by economy and politics, but the other stories that society and culture tell about the space are hidden behind boards, doors, shutters, and signs.

I think that it often takes the experience of one place to 'see' the potential of another. Looking at Elephant and Castle while researching La Goutte d'Or offers comparative reflections on the role of architecture and urban design production and policies in the shaping of a neighbourhood's present and future disposition. In looking at the differences and contextual singularities of the two neighbourhoods, it is important to understand that redevelopment does not always mean demolition or displacement. Demolition not only affects, physical structures but threatens relationships and solidarities; and many of the social, cultural and economic activities that are visible to the public eye happen thanks to infrastructures and practices that operate in the background. One cannot exist without the other.

     Fani Kostourou

What's the Worth of It All?

John Bingham-Hall

Welcome to La Goutte d'Or, a Parisian neighbourhood behind the Gare du Nord whose name – meaning 'the drop of gold' – belies its scruffy appearance and less-than-glittering reputation.[1] My colleague and I are here to meet Fayaz, a tailor and dressmaker, in his atelier, which lies behind an unmarked entrance on a backstreet corner. He greets us from behind his sewing machine and stays there throughout our visit, never losing contact with the garment-in-progress beneath his hands. We perch on stools by frosted windows that block the view from the street. With orders for the fabrication of stage costumes, runway pieces and event finery, from opera houses to fashion houses and individuals, there are no tables free of fabric, threads or machinery in the compact space. This is the urban backstage, where work happens away from the public eye and where the messiness of production is valued above carefully staged display.

Before we have a chance to make our inquiries, Fayaz interrogates us: 'I'd like to know what your objective is … to understand what constructive relationship I can have to this process?' I tell him we are documenting the spaces where artists, artisans, musicians – cultural

producers, in other terms – do their work. Our aim, I explain, is to offer architects, planners and organisations a deeper understanding of how and where culture is produced in cities. He listens and nods, rightly weighing up our intentions and whether he should help us. When I tell him we specifically want to protect the infrastructures that allow people to work independently and outside of corporate structures, his enthusiasm is evident. As he listens intently, I explain our understanding of cultural infrastructure as a set of conditions that allow individuals to define their own ways of working, with access to spaces, materials, support systems, funding and supply chains, whatever they need to imagine and produce cultural forms. His response takes me aback, and hits at the exact reason we started this study in the first place: the understanding that having access to the infrastructures for cultural production is not just about making a living, but about living *well*, with a sense of social or even spiritual value to one's work. As Fayaz explains:

> *You've seen today how the global economy is under monopoly, and it's the big financiers who built themselves a network that shares most of the global profit. Pretty much everyone has to listen to them and to follow their model. That vision … screw it. It's me that chooses my model. I stopped my studies, and I learned a craft.[2] For me, that meant finding my freedom, because I don't have to look for someone to sell my knowledge to. I have a craft. I sell know-how.*

So, what are infrastructures that enable cultural production worth to a city and its inhabitants? Clearly, their value goes beyond the simple fact of being able to earn a living, as Fayaz's personal manifesto makes clear. In which case, what other kinds of value do they give rise to, and who benefits from it? These questions are at once crucial and difficult to answer in both London and Paris, the two neighbouring but divergent global cities of our study, where globalised, finance-led economies and real estate pressures mean affordable space for independent cultural producers like Fayaz is far from guaranteed. But despite the neoliberalising project of current president Emmanuel Macron, the value system shaping France's cultural policy is different to that of the UK, and within it are developing approaches that are worth learning from. As we took our

1   Social studies of the neighbourhood acknowledge the predominance of negative media representations and even the label of 'ghetto' (see Bacqué and Fijalkow 2006, for example) that has helped La Goutte d'Or resist some of the gentrification that has been so dominant in other comparable neighbourhoods in the north and east of the city. Its 'scruffiness' derives as much from a historical lack of investment in public space as from the current frenzy of road works aiming to bring the neighbourhood into line with Paris's coherent urban aesthetic.

2   Originally *métier*, which in English denotes both *trade* and *craft*. Whereas in English, the former can be read with a derogatory overtone in comparison to the latter, in French the two render as equals, in language at least.

John Bingham-Hall

fieldwork from London to Paris, we observed investment in social infrastructures helping craftspeople like Fayaz to build their livelihoods through networks of collaboration, without the need for physical regeneration of their neighbourhood. Further afield, Marseille offers a counterpoint to both capital cities: an urban landscape where an abundance of space leads to a different set of value propositions. As the Greater London Authority (GLA) looks to develop tools for measuring social value and 'good growth' to guide its investment in cultural infrastructures, we will look here to projects in both Paris and Marseille that offer alternative definitions and mechanisms for the value of cultural infrastructure.

Economic value: making it pay

The GLA's Cultural Infrastructure Map offers a survey of London's artist ateliers, fashion and jewellery workshops, recording and rehearsal studios, performance and social spaces, and much more.[3] The cluster of Colombian-owned businesses in Elephant and Castle – cafés, restaurants, and nightclubs but also fashion designers and Latin beauty specialists – do not feature on it. These businesses cultivate 'sensorial infrastructures' – recipes, sounds and ways of gathering – that sustain a rich set of Latin American communities in this neighbourhood. However, sitting outside the government's definition of 'creative industries'[4] that have come to rival financial services for the position of London's dominant economic sector, they tend to be overlooked for the investment more formally defined creative industries have received in recent years.

The value of a vibrant migrant community to the wellbeing of its members, and the support system it provides to new arrivals, is hard to measure. This is especially the case in the financialised economy of the UK (and most other highly developed capitalist countries), where the definition of success for all kinds of enterprise is the production of surplus economic value, allowing payouts to shareholders. As economist Mariana Mazzucato has argued in her book *The Value of Everything*, an economy driven by this narrow idea – of value measured by profit – is one that will consistently and inevitably fail to solve the grand

social and environmental challenges bound to eventually undermine it.[5] The informal social services provided by Latin American businesses in Elephant and Castle *do* have an economic value, as they fill gaps in state provision caused by the failings that Mazzucato points to. But when the value system guiding public investment in all kinds of infrastructure – road, rail, broadband, or even artist workspaces – is purely in terms of the economic growth it drives, these stories of solidarity and cultural meaning never make it onto the balance sheet.[6]

Nevertheless, the GLA is attempting to make these value systems add up. Their Good Growth Fund offers grants to arts organisations and local authorities, supporting the development of retail spaces, social facilities, creative hubs and related public realm upgrades, such as those attached to the Hotel Elephant creative hub on Spare Street in Elephant and Castle. Wherever there is investment, though, there is a value proposition. In return for supporting arts organisations to create backstage infrastructure for artists, the GLA expects to see public-facing, onstage improvements that will help attract visitors and other commercial activities to neighbourhoods that are judged as underdeveloped, particularly if they are home to 'dirty' forms of economy like the car garages that Hotel Elephant replaced. There is no secret or hidden agenda here. The Good Growth Fund is exactly what it says on the tin: a fund to drive economic growth in London via 'good'

3   Greater London Authority (2019), "Cultural Infrastructure Map" [https://www.london.gov.uk/what-we-do /arts-and-culture/cultural-infrastructure -toolbox/cultural-infrastructure-map].

4   Department for Culture, Media and Sport (2001), "Creative Industries Mapping". Defined in UK Government policy as 'those industries which have their origin in individual creativity, skill and talent and which have the potential for wealth and job creation through the generation and exploitation of intellectual property'.

5   Mazzucato, M. (2018) *The Value of Everything: Making and Taking in the Global Economy*.

6   Tribillon, J., Bingham-Hall, J. (2020) "L'essor de la notion de cultural infrastructure urbaine". *Journal des anthropologue*s, 162163, pp. 47–64.

activities like culture, social enterprise, and public life that evidently bring value beyond the monetary. But this very same growth, and the gentrification it drives, risks destroying the value in the kinds of cultural infrastructures our study has documented in Elephant and Castle.

Social value: measuring the unmeasurable For the success of the 'good' to be mesured alongside the 'growth', social value must be quantified. In response to this challenge, organisations in both London and Paris are developing ways to measure social value. The GLA has commissioned urban practice We Made That and research centre LSE Cities to develop tools for measuring the social value of London's high streets. The *High Streets for All* report aims to help guide public investment in streets and the social and cultural infrastructures they are home to. The report demonstrated that meeting up with friends and family, using libraries and sports centres, or just enjoying the local neighbourhood were all equally important activities as shopping for the people interviewed in places like Lewisham town centre and Lower Clapton Road, on everyday streets not usually thought of as cultural destinations. It might sound obvious to anyone who enjoys living in an urban neighbourhood that high streets and cultural spaces are worth more than commerce, but for this kind of common sense to stand up in the calculations that drive infrastructure investment, social value has to be expressed in the same language as economic value.

In a more recent book, *Mission Economy*, Mazzucato proposes to turn the equation around. What if, instead of trying to measure the unmeasurable, investment in businesses and infrastructures was led by a social mission, and its success judged on whether that mission has been achieved? Mazzucato's proposed missions are concrete, if lofty (a hundred carbon-neutral cities by 2030, or a plastic-free ocean, for example), but the logic can be applied to cultural infrastructures too. France's *tiers lieux*– hybrid cultural centres focused spaces – are attempting to do just this. In Marseille, we met the coordinators and residents of Coco Velten, a dense warren of backstage workshops and offices with a public canteen, assembly room and rooftop garden, occupying a defunct administrative building belonging to the regional government. What makes this project unique among others in our study is its inclusion of emergency housing for refugees and asylum seekers. Whilst Coco Velten generates income from charging affordable rent to creative producers and businesses (and selling a lot of beer, as we were told), its aim is not to boost the local economy. Its self-stated mission, rather, is to fight against exclusion from housing and culture by providing free access to both and encouraging interaction between the two.

Tiers lieu means 'third space', and the projects falling under this umbrella are nodes where interests of the state, commerce and social action meet, sometimes awkwardly. Coco Velten enjoys free use of the publicly-owned building it occupies, as well as some basic state funding for its operation, but relies heavily on its own ability to generate revenue. *Tiers lieux* ('third spaces' in the plural) are much more financially independent of state support than more traditional arts centres, which are well-funded but subject to top-down interference. As a result, they have freedom in their operation, unlike fully state-funded arts centres whose agendas are highly influenced by central government. This freedom favours politically left-leaning self-organised urban collectives, but also happens to suit the current neoliberal government in its aim to shrink the state and its support for culture. A curious correspondence of values between opposing political movements has meant an explosion of opportunities to run *tiers lieux*, and a transformation of those self-organised collectives into large, corporate non-profits. Private landlords and public authorities alike see the value of protecting empty assets while supporting virtuous-seeming, socially-driven projects, but the risk is that these landlords have a different idea of value – that is, real estate value – that *tiers lieux* help to protect and even grow over time.

In response to this issue, Plateau Urbain established Commune Mesure, a research initiative inviting managers of *tiers lieux* to report their missions and how they are achieving them, in order to 'reveal virtuous practices' in a situation in which 'we struggle to take account of positive

impacts [of cultural infrastructures] because they don't fit within classic measures, usually centred on economic profitability.'[7] The projects that have responded to the call for contribution from Commune Mesure most commonly describe the missions of their projects with the words 'conviviality', 'creativity', 'cooperation', and 'welcome'.[8] In a country where the notion of *vivre ensemble* – living harmoniously alongside one another as neighbours, particularly in dense and diverse urban environments – is a national obsession, to the point of having its own governmental 'mission',[9] such a focus on solidarity and connection is not surprising. What is striking is the relative absence of artistic experimentation as a value in itself. The offer of subsidised workspaces at Coco Velten and other *tiers lieux* are predicated not on the inherent value of the work they support, but on the social value asked in return. As one product designer told us, 'The deal with Coco is to work … with the locals. And I'd like to, but it's super complicated.' Their small office is a place to 'think', but it lacks space for tools and messy material experimentation, or for welcoming the public. 'You need to give all participants the right tools, like a soldering iron, and I don't have that,' the product designer explained, 'or there's not enough money … And obviously I need to earn a living. Blocking time and money to do projects with locals, it's not easy.'

Tiers lieux, then, illustrate how different value propositions can overlap and even be in conflict within cultural infrastructure. Organisations such as Plateau Urbain and Yes We Camp are driven by the social mission of their work. Their rapid growth, however, is driven by the values of others: public bodies seeing a cheap way to provide cultural infrastructure, and landlords eyeing the potential value uplift in their properties brought by temporary projects that can be ejected when the conditions for redevelopment are right. Commune Mesure is an attempt to convince both figures that *tiers lieux* should not be confined to short-term experimentation before traditional development comes in, but that adaptability, independence and responsiveness should be permanent values built into the urban fabric. So, what about the value to independent cultural producers themselves — artists, craftspeople, designers and so on? Their less-than-commercial rents come at a hidden cost – the labour of free social services and cultural inclusion work, which many are unprepared and untrained for the realities of, and which would cost city authorities dearly to provide professionally. This is not to say that *tiers lieux* are not incredibly important and valuable experiments in city-making: making arguments for the recycling of the built environment, resisting carbon-heavy demolition and redevelopment, and testing new kinds of hybridity and exchange between different parts of society. What they demonstrate is the importance of paying attention not just to how *much* social value there is in cultural infrastructure, but *who* is producing it and *who* is benefitting from it.

The invaluable: independence, experimentation, taking a nap

To see what infrastructure looks like when it makes a value proposition directly to artists, you need to look a little further to the north of Marseille, to KLAP Maison pour la danse. Michel Kelemenis, KLAP's founder, never intended to establish a space for cultural production, let alone one with a mission. Instead,

7   Commune Mesure (2022), 'Les mots de l'évaluation' [the translation is mine] [https://communemesure.fr/].

8   Taken from analysis of data from Commune Mesure performed in Drumm, E., Sadekar, O. (2022) *Tiers-Lieux: comparing the way places define themselves and how they are talked about on Twitter.* [https://sadekar-onkar.github.io/tierslieux_ddps/].

9   Ministère de la Culture, 'Mission Vivre Ensemble' (2004), [https://www.culture.gouv.fr/Thematiques/Developpement-culturel/Le-developpement-culturel-en-France/Mission-Vivre-Ensemble].

What's the Worth of It All?

the project emerged out of necessity and was shaped around his own choreographic process. The rehearsal studio he had built for himself, in an industrial building in the northern suburbs of Marseille, was often empty, so he began to rent it cheaply or lend it to other young choreographers in the city. In 2009, the site was requisitioned by the city government for a school, and so the municipality undertook the task of finding a new site for an expanded facility for exactly the hosting and sharing Kelemenis had instinctively been doing. The chosen site, a defunct milking shed, would become a purpose-built facility for dance creation, hosting *Kelemenis et Cie* (the choreographer's own artistic company) as well as short-term residencies for other companies and individuals. Like Coco Velten and many other *tiers lieux*, KLAP relies on free space, in a city where vacancy of industrial space has been more of a problem than real estate pressure. Unlike *tiers lieux*, though, where a social mission is the principal value and cultural production is there to support it, dance itself is the driver behind KLAP, and production is prioritised over performance. 'We have performance capacities ... but the fundamental idea is to support creation,' a staff member told us. The dance artists we spoke to were all being offered free studio space for residencies ranging from two to four weeks. Instead of the demand for informal social services in return, they felt their work was valued in its own right. This situation is rare, even for dance, where residencies are usually given in return for some form of public engagement, which may only be 'onstage' for one hour, but that takes days of backstage planning and preparation. Residencies also add an emotional strain, as a young queer-identifying choreographer with a Marseille-based company told us: 'Yo them [cultural institutions], it becomes *the* important thing ... And in fact, this thing becomes super time-consuming, and it's my time of research, my time of fragility, of accepting getting it wrong, of getting lost, of not

knowing, of taking naps, of leaving earlier. Because that's what creation is, it's a kind of time that you can't anticipate.'

For artistic creation, freedom of time and space are of the utmost value. We spoke to another choreographer, after watching her performance which used reimagined baroque costumes to accentuate everyday contemporary gestures and draw attention to their theatricality. This work was the result of a long series of production-focused residencies, including ones at KLAP. She described the protection that KLAP offered from the constant demands of display, allowing her time to process the intense experience of travelling through the busy city as an artist attuned to bodies and movement. Her work offered these experiences back as part of the material for her entrancing performances. Allowing for this long process requires trust in the value of these offerings, in the ability of dance to act as a mirror on our own bodies, and in the possibilities of their ways of relating to each other and themselves. This is the kind of trust that is hard to see in *tiers lieux*, where artistic production is not an end in itself but a means towards producing other kinds of value.

KLAP is a unique case, combining long-term stability with the independence of *tiers lieux*. But this enviable situation does hide another set of values. While KLAP was not initiated by the city government, the location it was offered is no accident. It forms part of the Euroméditerrannée zone, a public-private regeneration project focused on the typically working-class, post-industrial hinterland of Marseille's port. Though the site itself is not temporary, as its location was not viewed as valuable for redevelopment at the time, it was still implanted in a deprived location with the expectation that investment in a permanent, landmark piece of dance infrastructure would help build a cultural reputation for the regeneration area.[10] This creates a tension for KLAP's artists, who feel protected by the cocoon of the

10 The staff we spoke to also credit this uniquely stable situation, and the investment it received, to the personal charisma and tenacity of Michel Kelemenis, as well as the respect he is viewed with as an artist at a local scale.

John Bingham-Hall

dance studios but isolated from their surroundings, and doubtful of the viability of the organisation's attempts to reach out to its neighbours via the education programmes demanded as part of the programme funding it receives from the regional government. 'It's a very luxurious place in a poor neighbourhood,' one artist told us. 'It's not embedded in the neighbourhood, even though they tried.'

KLAP is part of a web of value propositions: trust on behalf of its founder, an artist himself, in the inherent value of artistic creation; a municipality hoping to show the value in a wider neighbourhood; and a state increasingly demanding more value in return for the shrinking funding it offers. The freedom it offers to artists is invaluable, but it is still based on the idea that new cultural infrastructure is needed to bring value to a neighbourhood rich with overlooked forms of production. Fayaz and his fellow tailors in La Goutte d'Or offer a counterpoint to this complex, showing how the infrastructure of cooperation can support the freedom of the already existing. La Fabrique de La Goutte d'Or is a legally incorporated cooperative, assembling a number of independent tailors with other small fashion-related businesses. Depending on who you ask, the structure was either initiated by the tailors themselves or by city hall, but in either case, the latter had a clear interest in supporting it. By providing funding to help establish a non-profit organisation (an *association loi 1901*) that would administer the collective, supporting with bureaucratic processes of invoicing and employment law that many of the neighbourhood's craftspeople did not know how to complete, the city government was aiming to formalise La Goutte d'Or's economy. In the process, its economy became visible and measurable, enabling politicians to show they were 'normalising' a neighbourhood that was viewed as a 'communitarian' ghetto, cut off from the state.[11] The politics of this, of course, can be debated.

The trade-off for France's more generous state funding for culture is also more state intervention and control. For the tailors participating, though, the cooperative means respect for, and valorisation of, their craft. The *association* interfaces with prestigious clients, taking orders for the production of costumes and collections from fashion houses and cultural institutions that the independent tailors would struggle to reach alone. These orders are shared around a network of producers with different jobs, or even different parts of the same job, being apportioned depending on their specific expertise: suiting, corsetry, millinery and so on. La Fabrique makes La Goutte d'Or's independent ateliers work a little like a distributed production line for high-end tailoring. The difference, that was so important to Fayaz, is that rather than selling their labour to  a corporate entity, they remain independent and free, holding onto the economic value their products bring them, but also the ownership and management of their crafts. They can take on other jobs, often fabricating outfits for special occasions in a range of traditional European or African tailoring styles, as well as innovative hybrids of both. La Fabrique allows the urban backstage of La Goutte d'Or to be appreciated, without being put on show. The skills concentrated here – deeply cultural and creative ones – are being noticed and paid for, but without needing to be turned into forms of cultural experience or even social services, as *tiers lieux* are under pressure to do in order to justify the support they receive. It also allows value to appreciate, to grow over time as relationships are built and connections are made within the neigh-

11   In France, the 'Republican ideal' is that all citizens should first and foremost be French. Staying within communities of ethnic or religious basis is denounced as communitarianism, and as an affront to this ideal. The reality, of course, is that this accusation is only levelled against racialised people and never against white or Christian communities.

bourhood. As Fayaz told us, he 'chose this neighbourhood because it's very rich, and it's rich because of diversity. We have all the nationalities of the world here. And that, with the basis of real economic development [enabled by La Fabrique], that's culture.' No landmark architectural gesture is needed to represent this richness, because its value is not based on how it looks but on what it makes possible.

The logic of value at play in the example of La Fabrique de La Goutte d'Or turns that dominant dynamic in London on its head. Rather than having to prove and quantify social value in order to survive, it shows how investment in the social infrastructure of cooperation can drive fairer economic development. Solidarity between the tailors of La Goutte d'Or is an infrastructure for, rather than an outcome of, the productive activities that characterise the neighbourhood. What is at stake is not *how much* value is produced there, but *who* benefits from it. There is nothing inherently wrong with growing a local economy in a place like La Goutte d'Or, or even measuring its monetary scale. The problem is growth and measurement for their own sake. The growth of value is described as appreciation, but we need to look carefully at *where* that appreciation is happening. Is it in property prices and international cultural cachet, or is it in the skills and wealth in the hands of a diverse community that welcomes new migrants and helps them in their first steps towards gaining a foothold in society? Appreciation also means paying attention to what is already there. The inequalities evident in Elephant and Castle – prioritising shiny new studios with landscaped public realm over the kinds of appreciation of value enjoyed by the tailors in La Goutte d'Or – shows the danger in letting appearances drive our understanding of the value of the urban backstage.

Stating *who* and *where* is critical in making value propositions that are honest and clear. It is unquestionable that Coco Velten and other *tiers lieux* create social value by offering free access to creative skills workshops in underprivileged communities and emergency housing in a culturally dynamic environment. To do so, though, value must be extracted from the creative producers working there, not just as rents but also in the form of time and energy. As KLAP showed us, time and energy are the primary resources for creative production. On the other hand, the price for KLAP's respect for the resources of artistic freedom is its difficulty connecting with its neighbourhood. This does not mean that KLAP has no social value and Coco Velten has no artistic value, but that value in each case is produced across different timescales and manifests in different places. KLAP places trust in the hope that protecting artistic experimentation will eventually lead to dance works that might subtly shift societal understanding of bodies and their meaning. Coco Velten places trust in the fact that opening up the process of production as a social resource will eventually lead to valuable forms of creative innovation. All these approaches can be important parts of a complex, dynamic urban backstage, but only if we appreciate the importance of making value clear.

The Stages

Cecily Chua

Introduction   Our selection of case studies was based on a fine-grained understanding of each city and neighbour-hood – through ethnographic exploration, interviews, tips, and knowledge from local creatives – rather than statistical or representational sampling. Each case study is illustrated by a series of detailed axonometric drawings that document the layout and architecture of each space, zooming in to show the life and objects that animate them.

In London, we focused on how the railway arch in Elephant and Castle had been adapted and reused by three very different cultural producers. In Glasgow, the post-industrial Barras Market gave us a mix of buildings to explore: industrial warehouses and vacant retail units, all home to a diverse mix of initiatives, from grassroots community-run projects to established creative workspace providers. No single neighbourhood can visibly embody Marseille's culture-led regeneration. The combination of strong public support at regional and national levels for cultural projects and the prevalence of vacant buildings dispersed across the city guided our selection of case studies.

London   Maldonado Walk is home to eight railway arches inhabited by a cluster of businesses run by the Latin American diaspora. The Walk was renamed in 2018 after the Ecuadorian scientist Pedro Vicente Maldonado to highlight the presence of Elephant and Castle's Latin community. Spare Street is a new workspace facility for artists and creative entrepreneurs. It is managed by Hotel Elephant and occupies five railway arches; rents from hotdesking space and private offices subsidise studio spaces for artists, designer-makers and creative start-ups. Robert Dashwood Way is a business park established in 1970. It contains a stretch of fifteen arches accommodating light industrial trades, including metal works, manufacturing, storage, and suppliers to some of London's major cultural institutions.

Glasgow   Many Studios offers forty-five workspaces to a community of over sixty people, from visual artists and designers to writers and engineers. Designed and managed by New Practice architects, the former storage warehouse was adapted into workspaces in 2016. The Space inhabits a former House of Fraser department store and is Scotland's first pay-what-you-decide community arts venue. It offers creative workspace, rehearsal rooms, community-focused social facilities, and support for the local homeless population. The Barras East End Studios (BEES) is a collective of former market traders based in a former warehouse situated between two of the Pipe Factory buildings. Opened in 2019, the BEES hosts traders that produce their own goods on-site.

Marseille   Coco Velten is a hybrid space that offers affordable work-space for artists and non-profit organisations alongside emergency housing for the homeless. It is a meanwhile project inhabiting a nineteenth-century building formerly used for public administration. Rue Léon Bourgeois is a narrow residential street with a cluster of small workshops in the garage spaces at the back. Some have been renovated as office spaces for small businesses in the creative industries, while others retain light industrial uses. KLAP Maison pour la danse opened in 2011. Previously a dairy shed, it was adapted into three purpose-built studio spaces for choreographic production, largely through an artist residency model, as well as spaces for some community-oriented education activities.

■ Case Studies
▨ Local Cultural Infrastructure

London

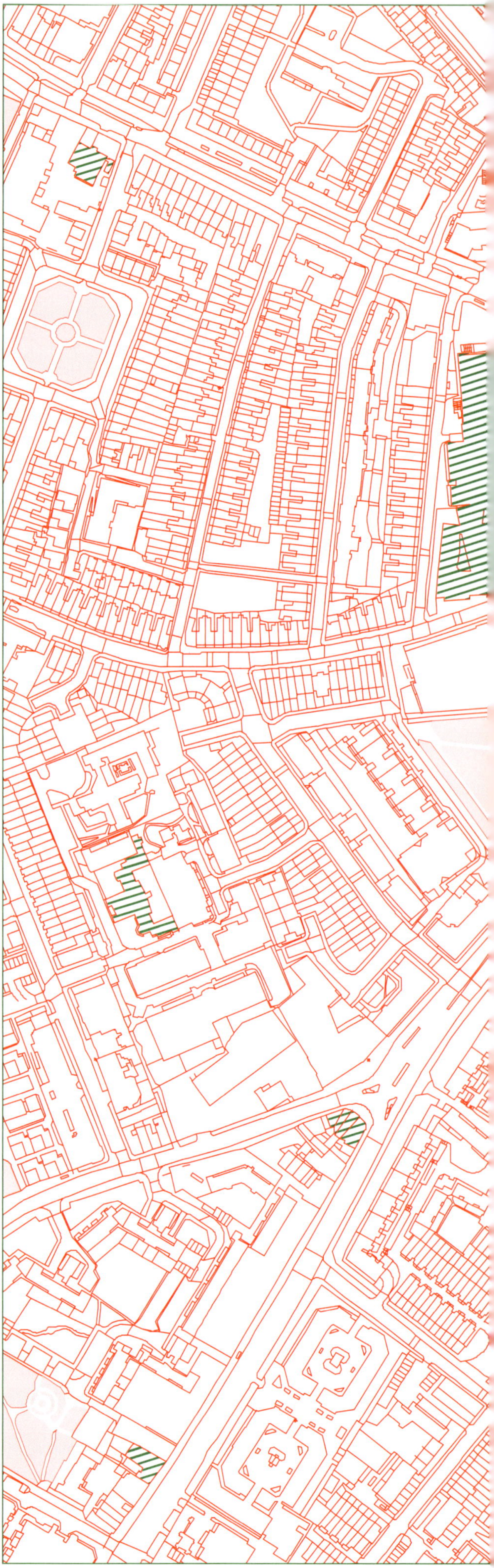

1. Maldonado Walk
2. Spare Street
3. Robert Dashwood Way

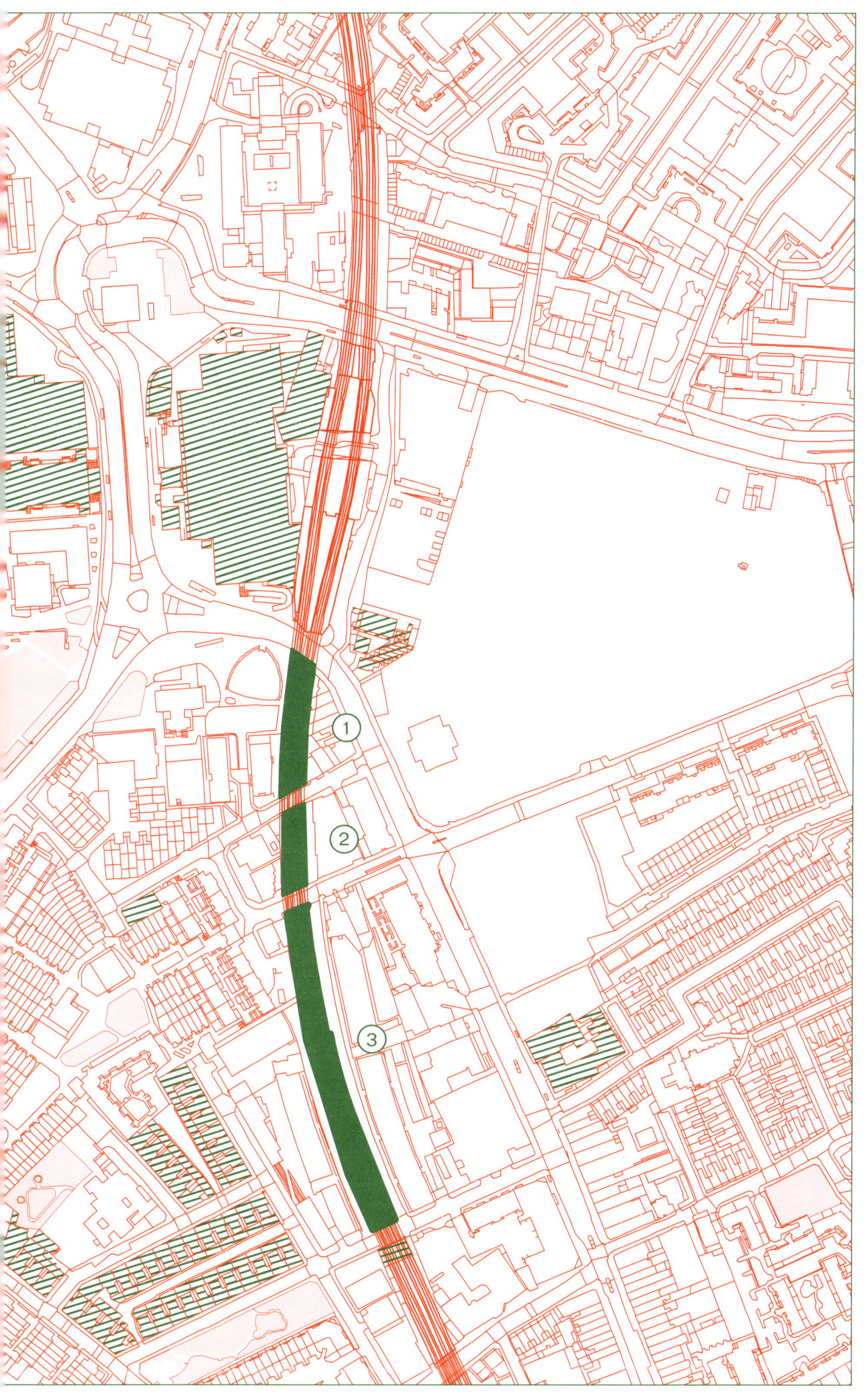

1
2
3

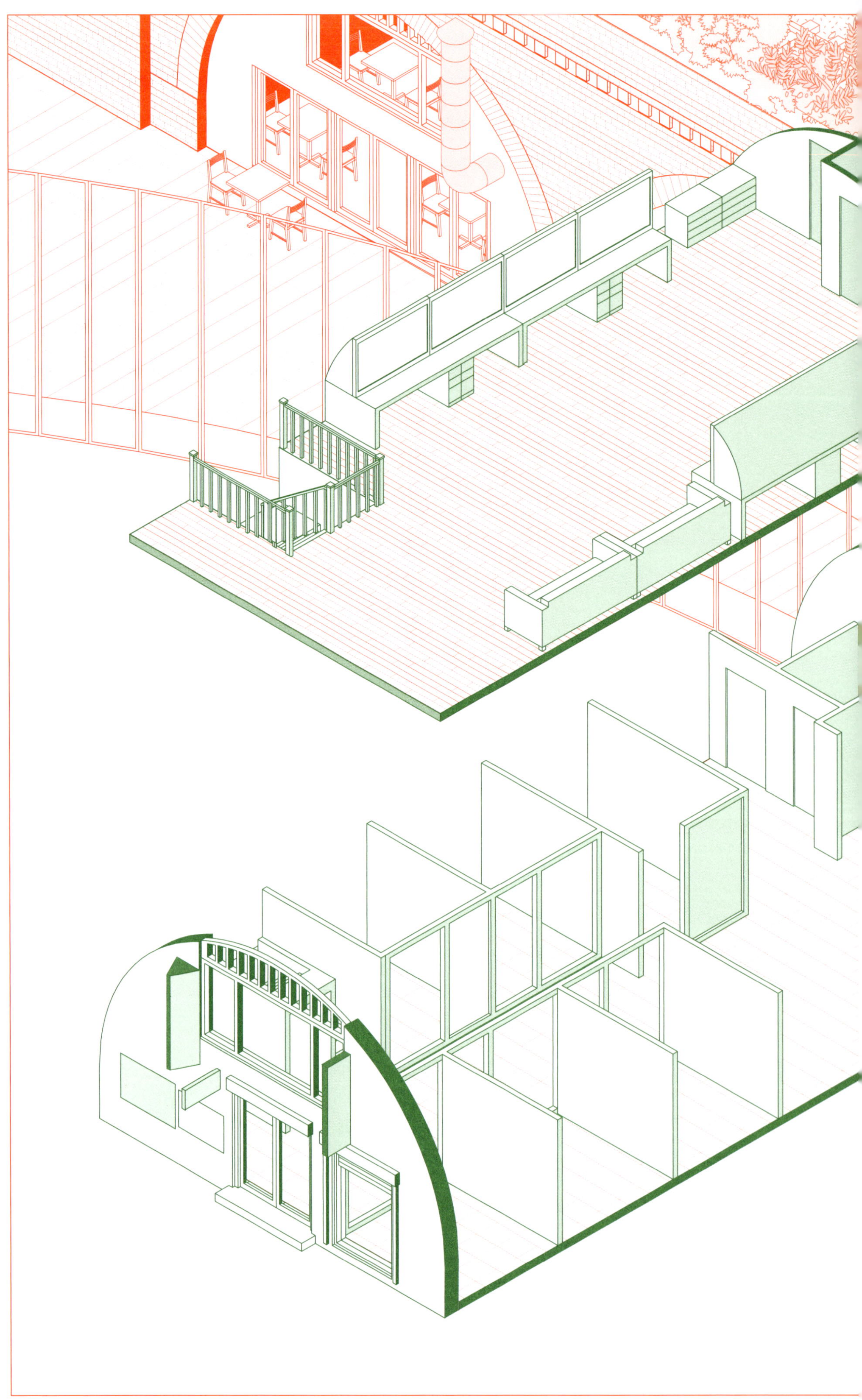

The Stages: London

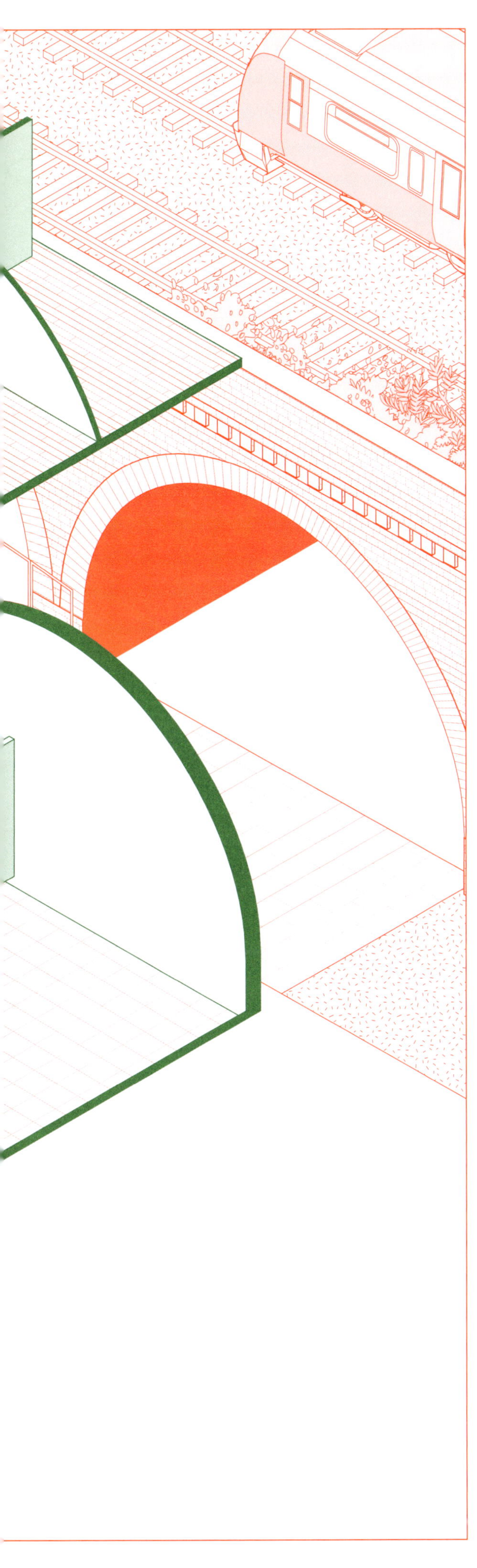

The Stages: London

The Stages: London

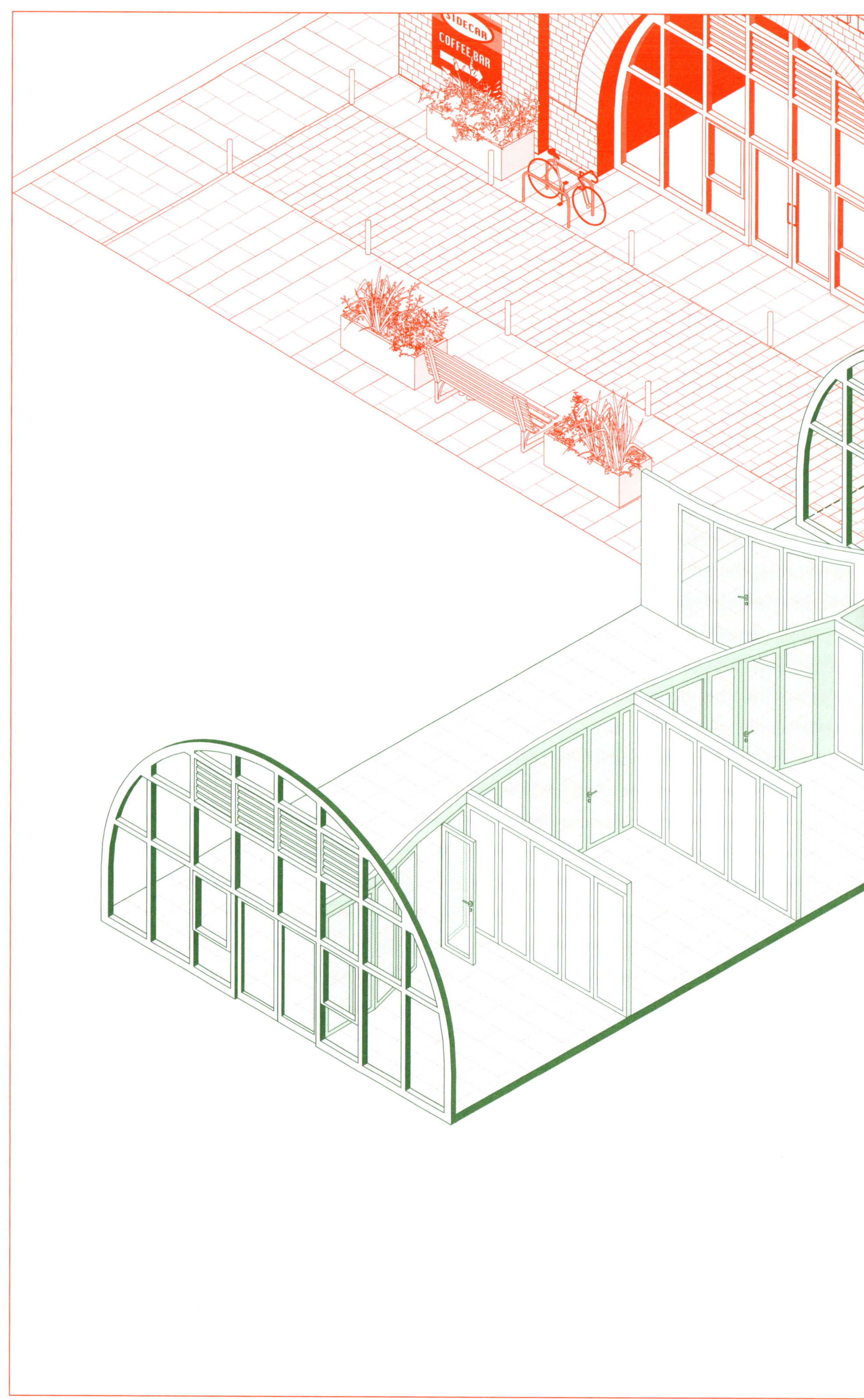

The Stages: London

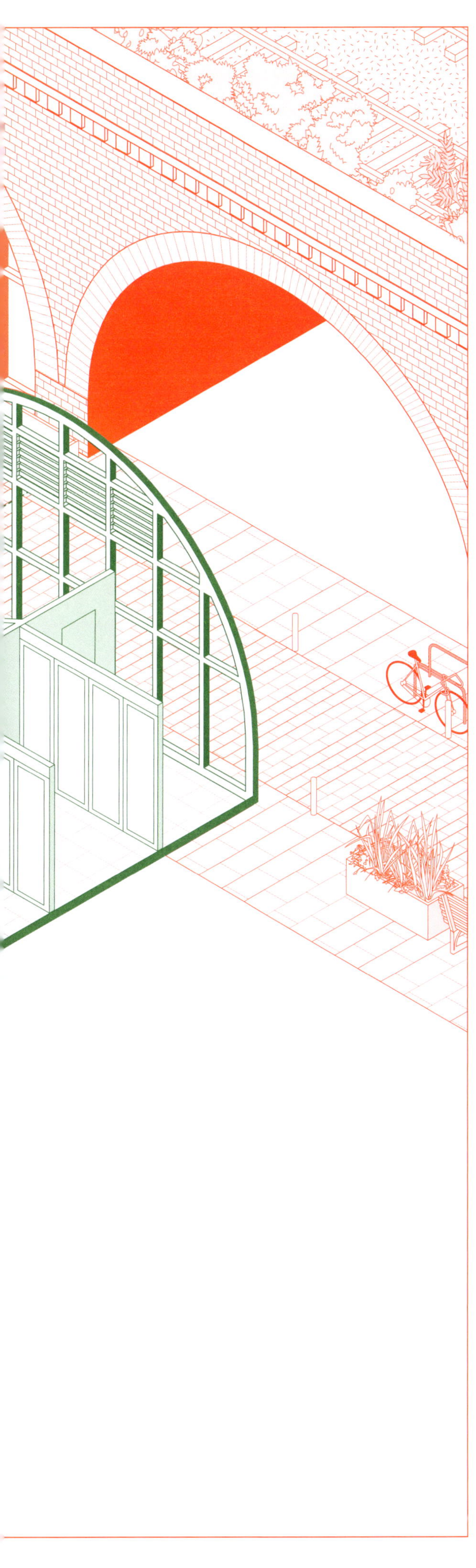

The Stages: London

The Stages: London

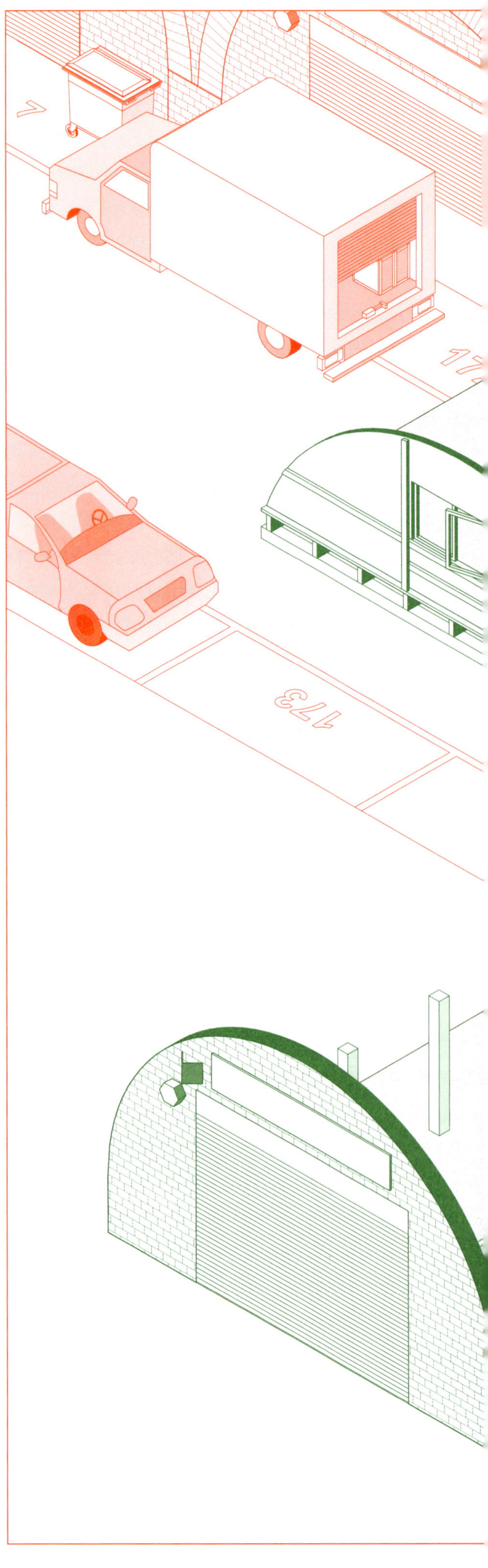

The Stages: London

174
175

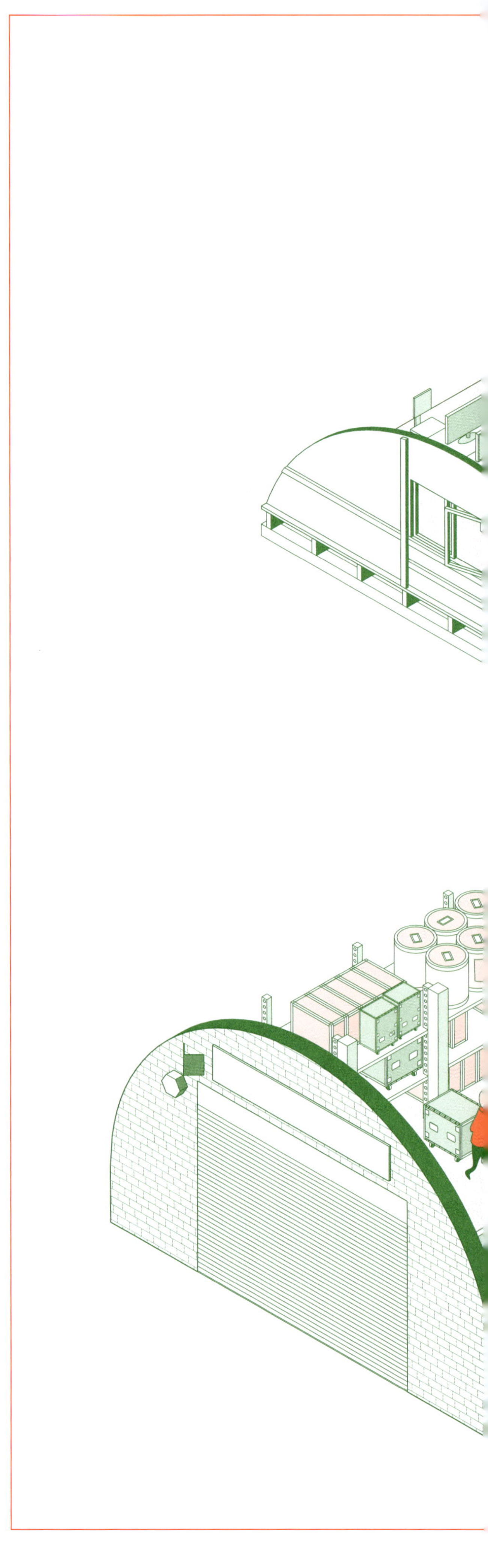

The Stages: London

V&A
barbican
NT

Glasgow

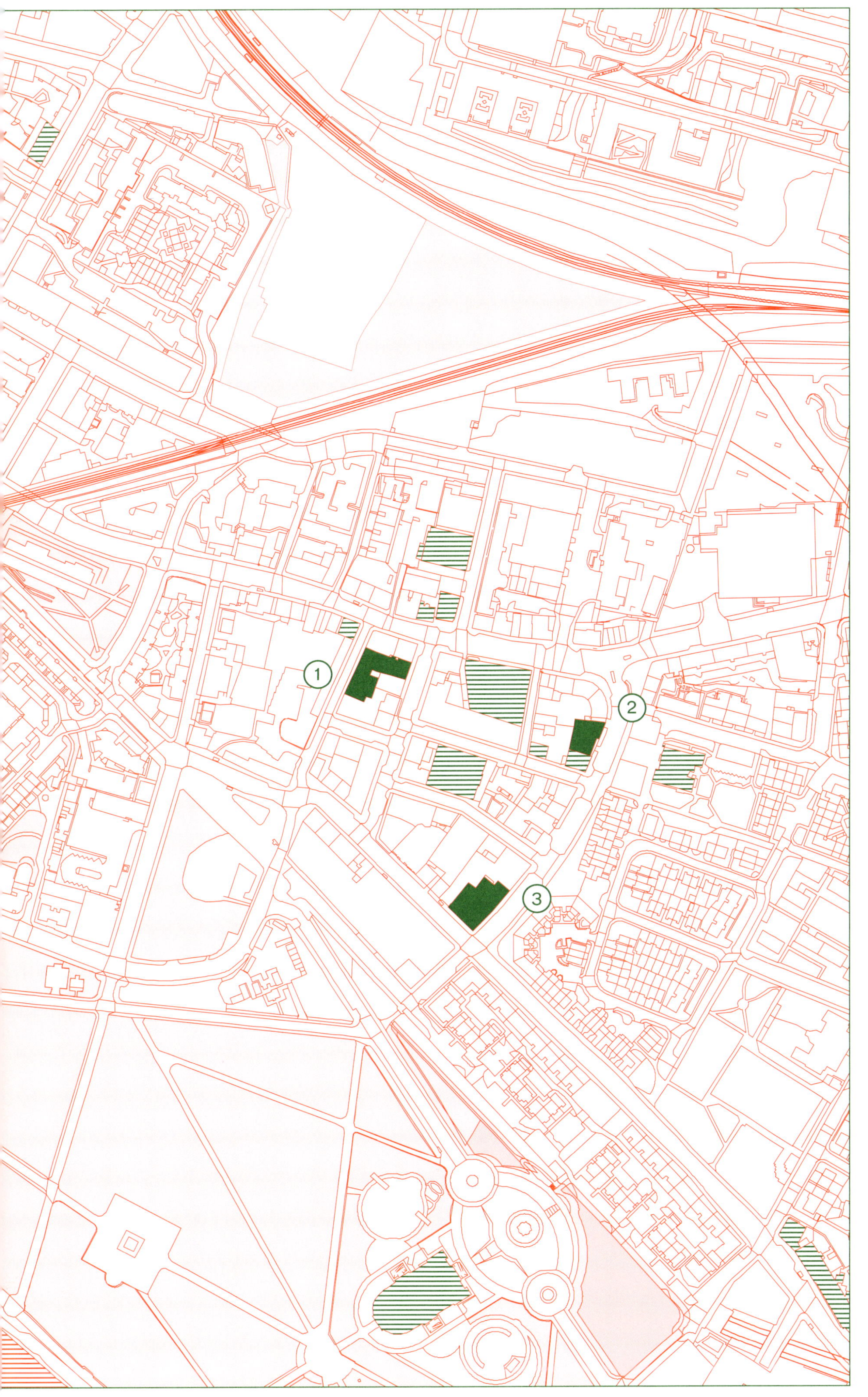

1
2
3

The Stages: Glasgow

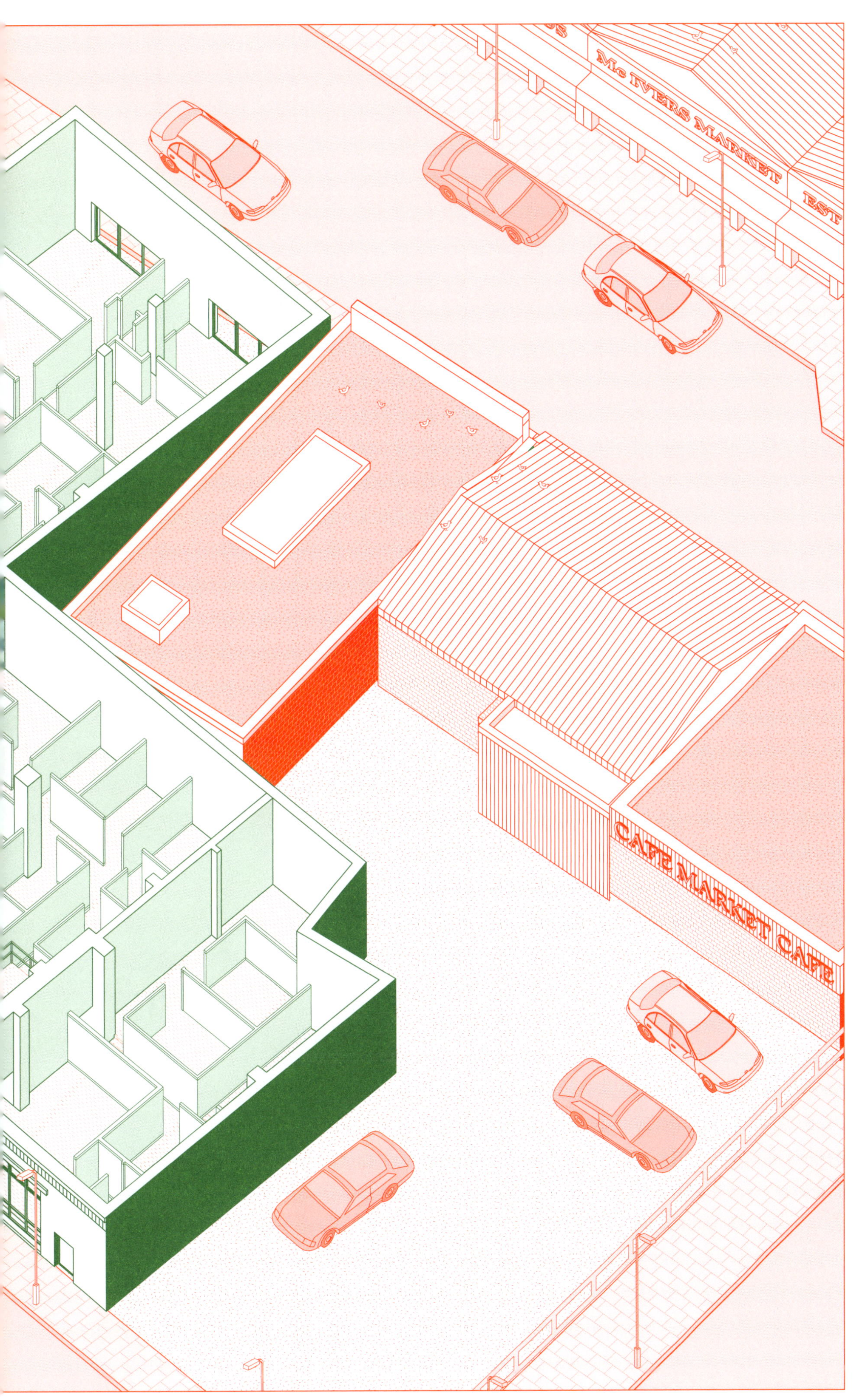

Mc IVERS MARKET
EST
CAFE MARKET CAFE

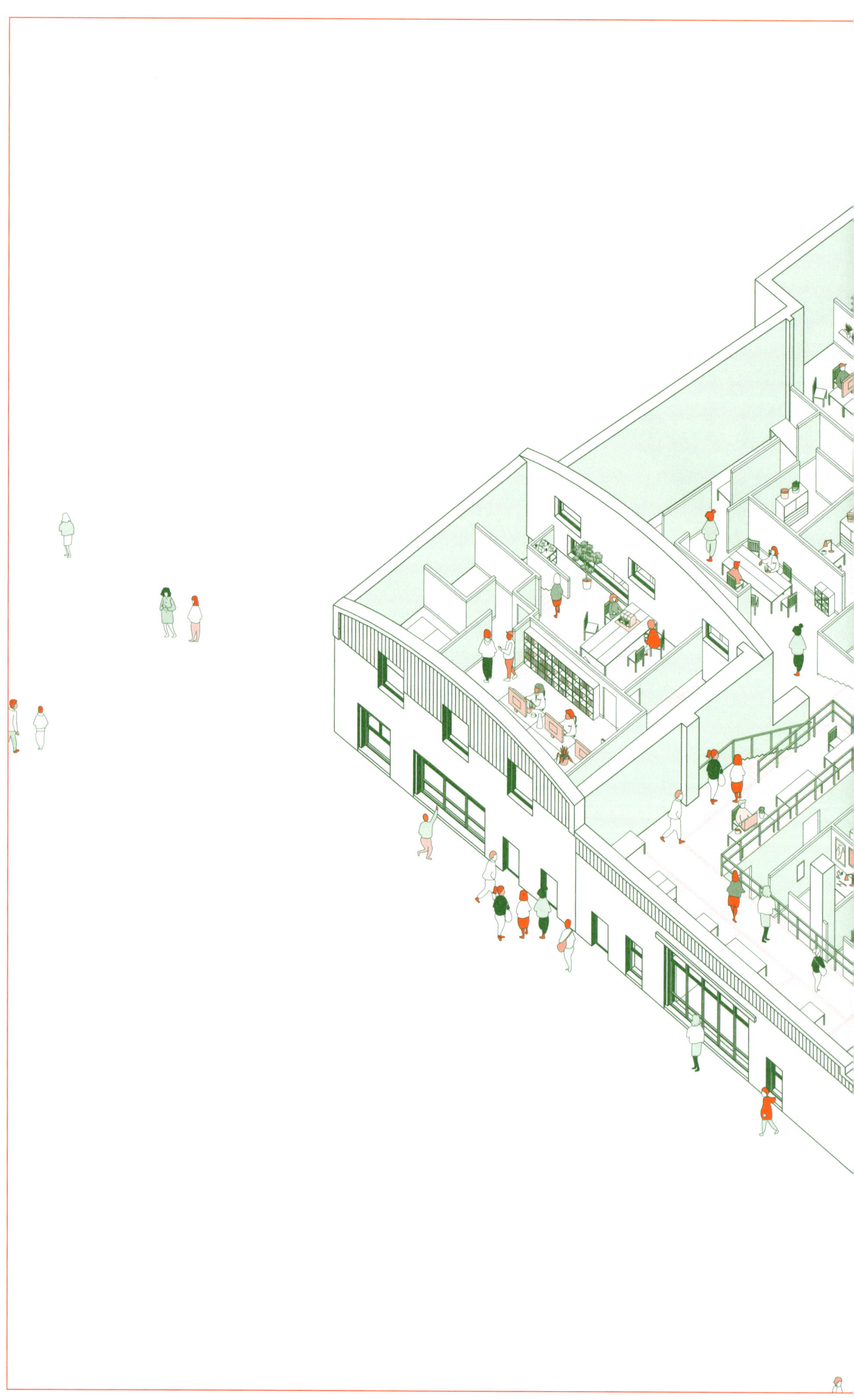

The Stages: Glasgow

The Stages: Glasgow

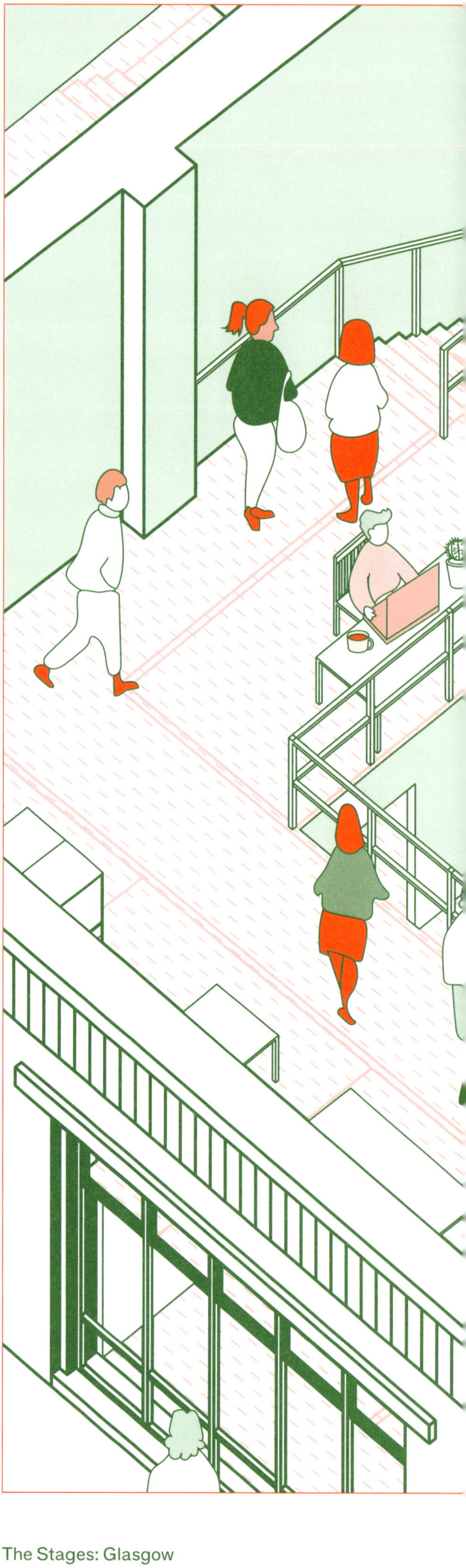

THE BARRAS
B.E.E.
36 BAINS ST
BY INDUSTRY WE...

BARRAS EAST END STUDIOS

The Stages: Glasgow

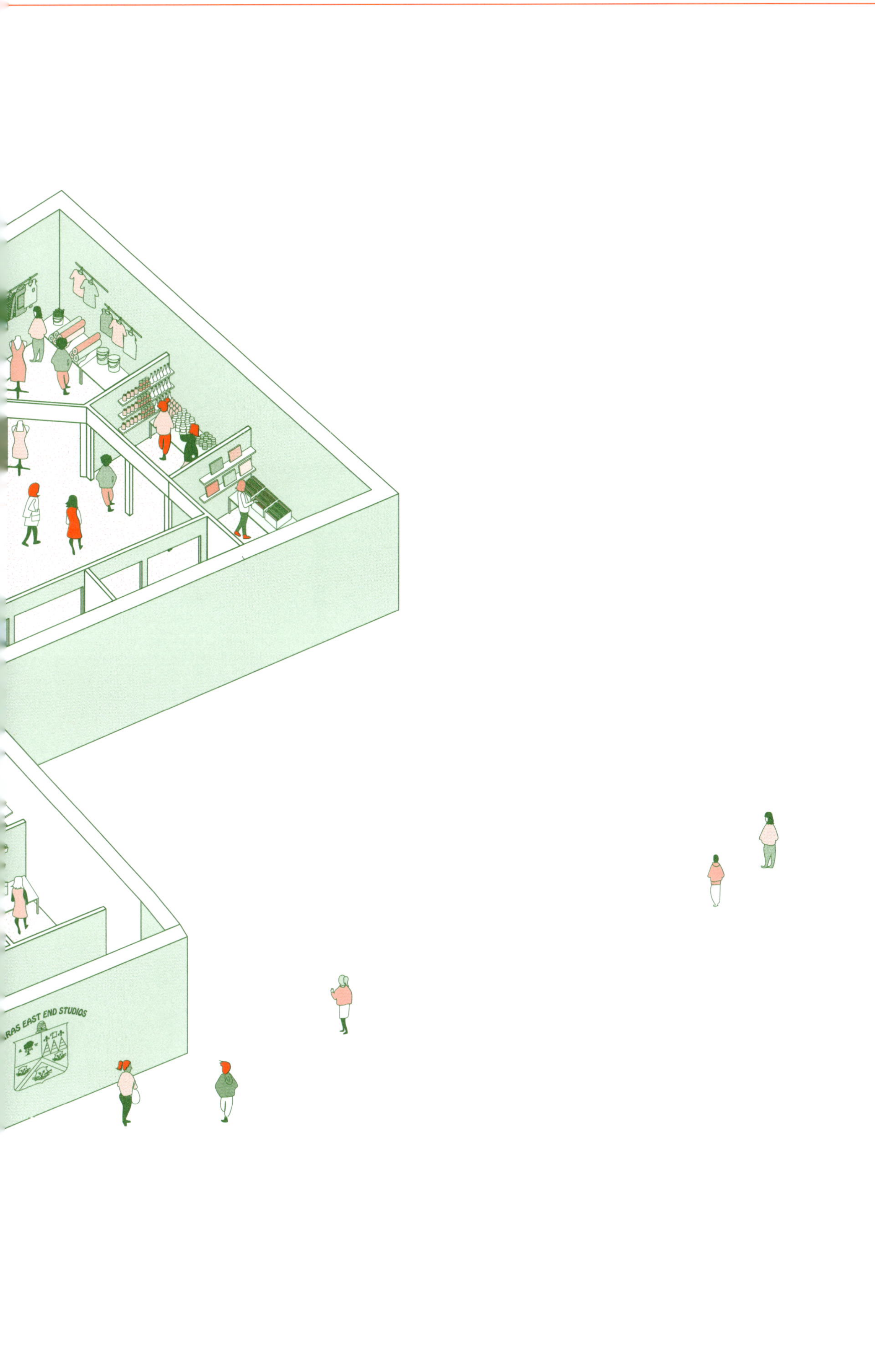
RAS EAST END STUDIOS

The Stages: Glasgow

BARRAS EAST END STUDIOS

The Stages: Glasgow

The Stages: Glasgow

The Stages: Glasgow

Marseille

① Coco Velten
② KLAP Maison pour la danse
③ Rue Léon Bourgeois

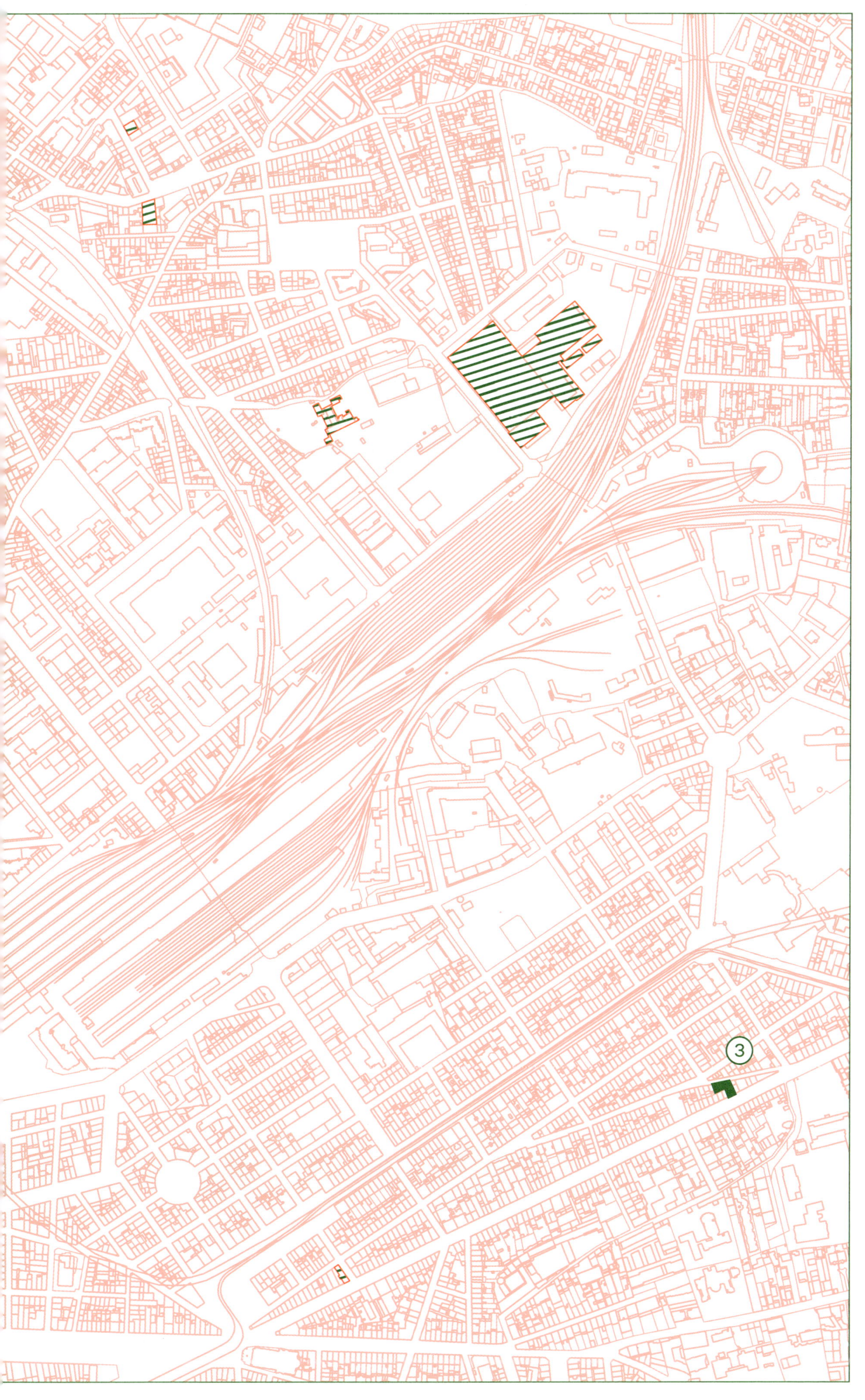

3

The Stages: Marseille

The Stages: Marseille

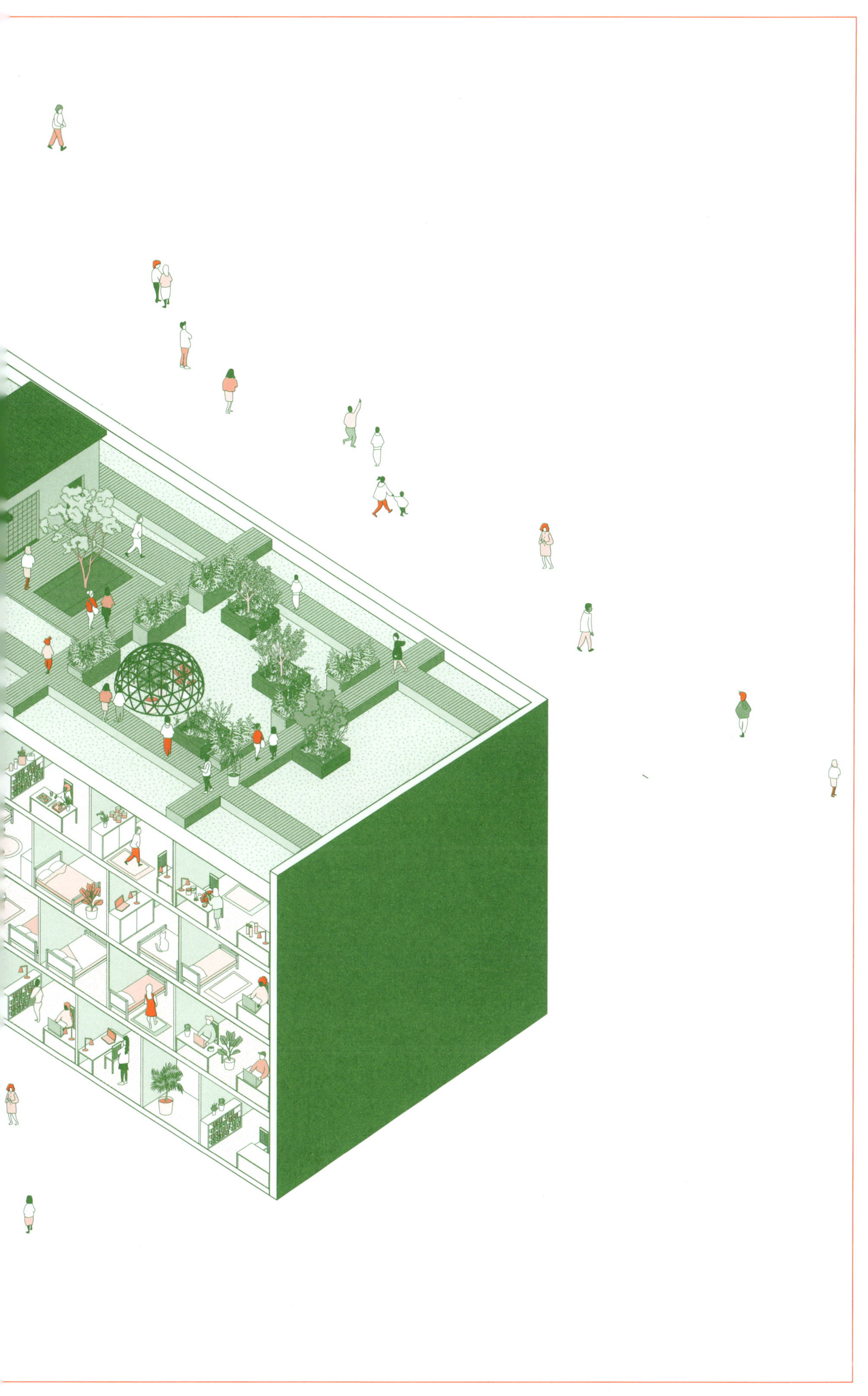

The Stages: Marseille

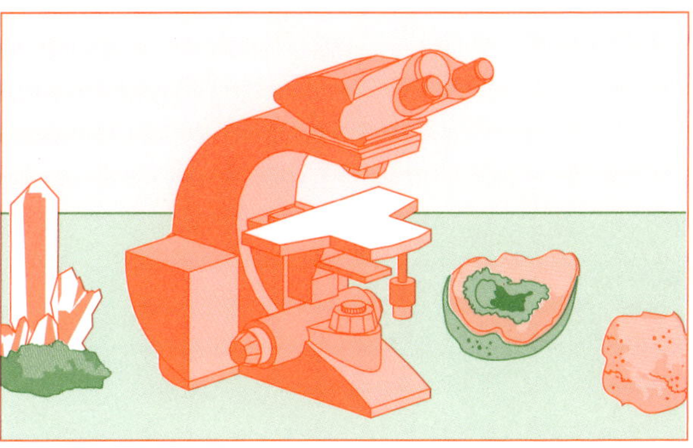

The Stages: Marseille

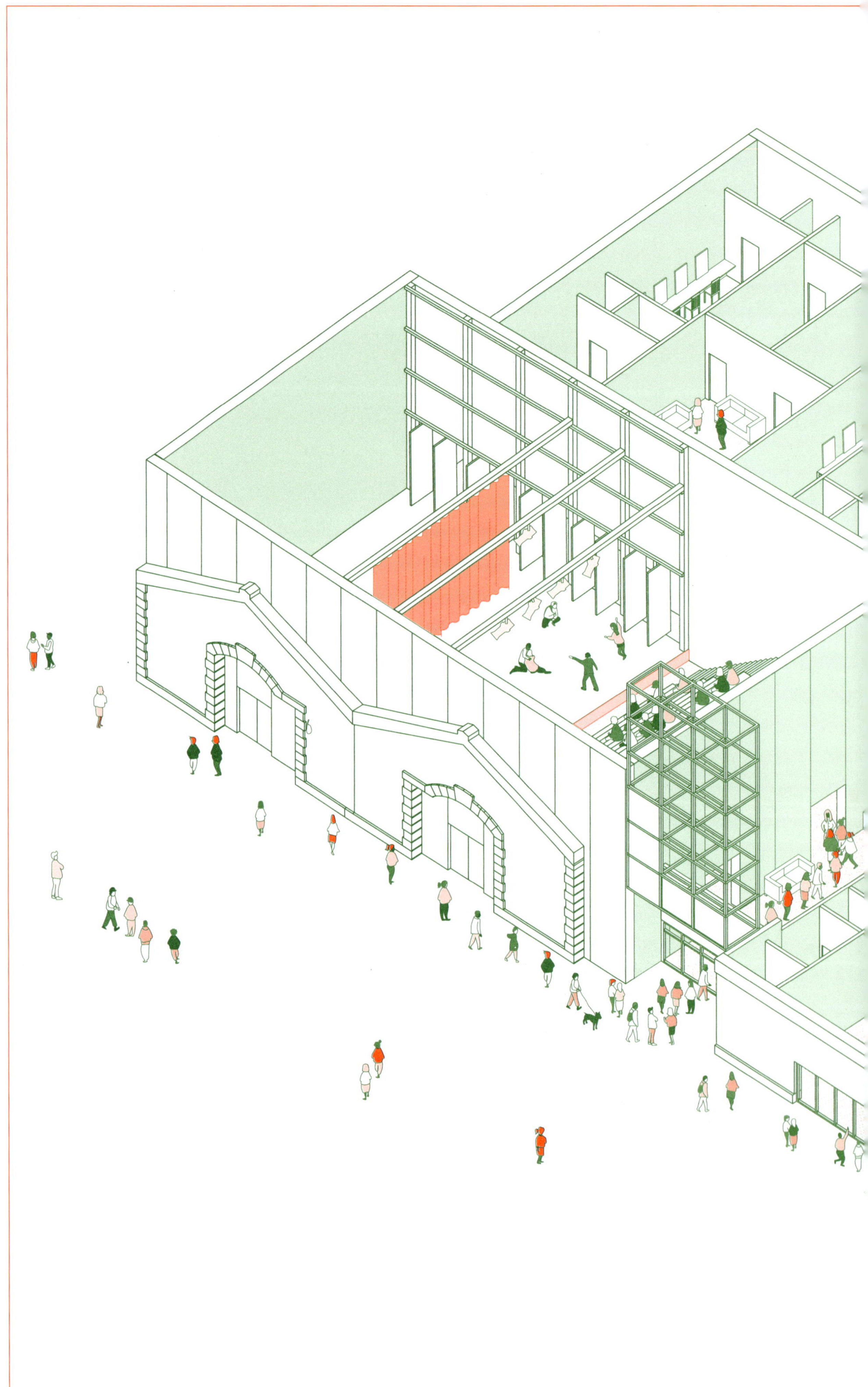

The Stages: Marseille

The Stages: Marseille

The Stages: Marseille

The Stages: Marseille

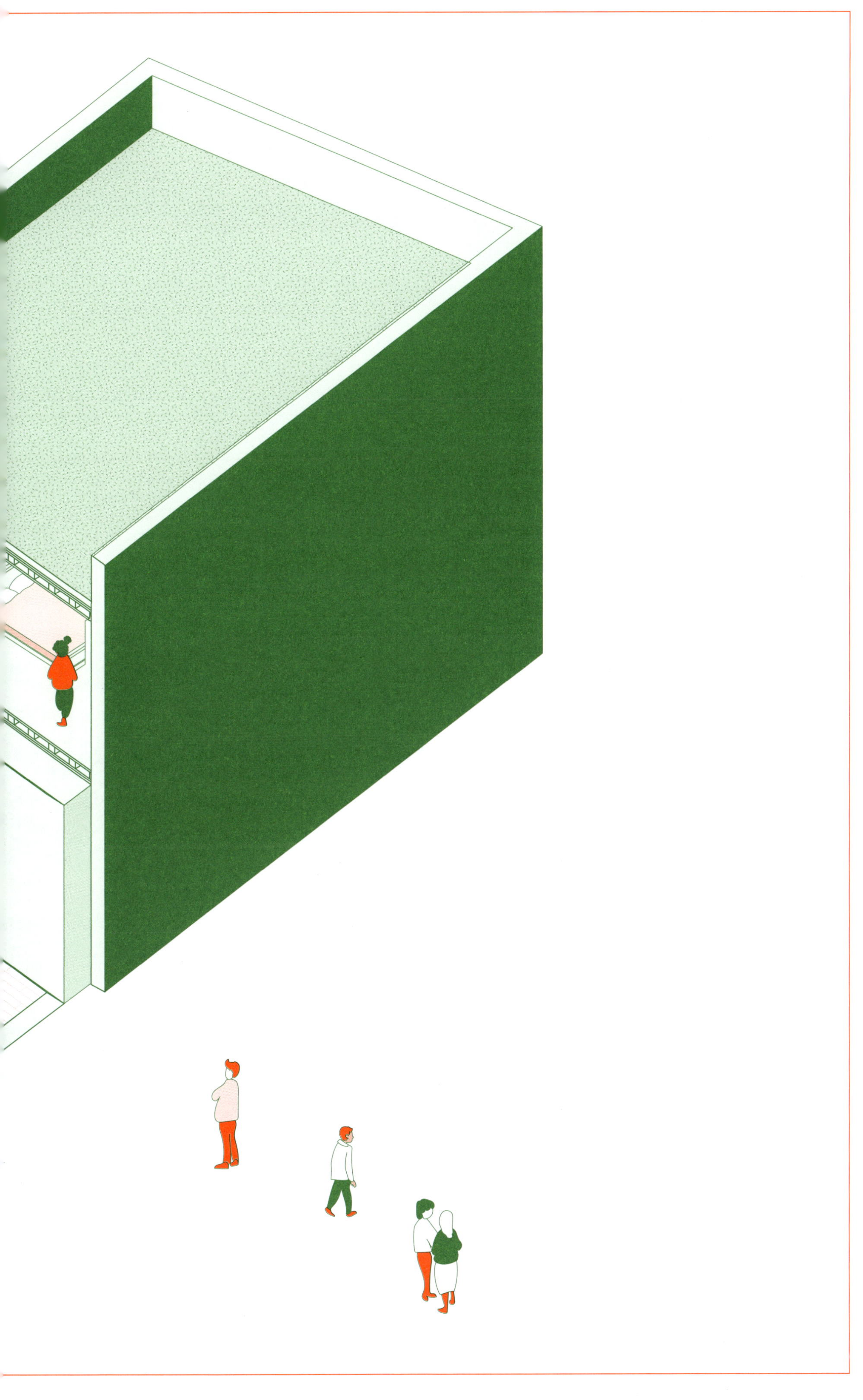

The Stages: Marseille

ANDREA CETRULO is a curator, sociologist and DJ, and has an affinity for architecture, philosophy, the Atlantic Ocean, and wine. She studied Sociology at the University of Barcelona, and Urban Studies at University College London. She shares her life-long fascination with the occult through her monthly show on Noods, a UK independent radio station.

CECILY CHUA is Director at Theatrum Mundi. She has a background in architecture (Royal College of Art), urban research and publishing. Her works focuses on the cultural life of our towns and cities, seeking to understand people's lived experiences of their urban environments and the subcultures that evolve from them. Her work has been exhibited internationally at the Architecture and Urbanism Biennales of Seoul, Buenos Aires, and Glasgow.

ELAHE KARIMNIA is a Senior Lecturer in Critical Urban Practice at the University of the West of England and Advisor at Theatrum Mundi. She is an urbanist and architect, engaged in research and teaching at the intersection of urban design and critical theory. She is interested in designing publicness through plural narratives and multiple temporalities. Elahe holds a PhD from KTH and has studied and worked in Tehran, Stockholm, Toronto, and London.

FANI KOSTOUROU is an Urban Computation Specialist at Grimshaw Architects. She is an architect and urbanist, holding a PhD from UCL Bartlett, and teaches at Cardiff University, the University for the Creative Arts, and Central Saint Martins. Kostourou conducts research, engages in curatorial and editorial work, and publishes internationally on design, computation, critical and interdisciplinary spatial theories, housing, and urban cultures.

JOHN BINGHAM-HALL is an Associate for European Projects at Theatrum Mundi and an independent researcher interested in performances, infrastructures, and technologies of shared life in the city. With a background in music (Goldsmiths) and architectural theory (UCL Bartlett), he works across artistic, spatial and critical humanities to question and participate in the making of the urban public sphere. Alongside initiating projects with Theatrum Mundi, he has collaborated on research projects at the London School of Economics and Oxford, taught at Central Saint Martins and University College London, published writing across scholarly and arts platforms, and organised queer cultural events.

LABEJA KODUA OKULLU is Publishing and Education Associate at Theatrum Mundi. He is a Ghanaian-British writer who lives in London. After studying English and Comparative Literature at Goldsmiths, he went on to complete The Novel Studio writing course at City, University of London, and is currently working on his first novel. Labeja has published poetry with *Forward Poetry* and *Rattle* magazine and essays with *The Smart Set* magazine.

MARCOS VILLALBA is a graphic designer and photographer born in Madrid. He graduated from Central Saint Martins in 2008 and spent the following decade working in London. He currently resides in Montevideo, Uruguay, where he runs a design studio working with clients across the fields of art, culture and education, as well as self-initiated projects focused on architecture and urbanism. He has collaboraed with Theatrum Mundi on digital projects, publications and exhibition design.

MARTA MICHALOWSKA is a curator, producer, artist and writer based in London. She recently completed her debut novel *Sketching in Ashes*, supported by Arts Council England through the Developing Your Creative Practice programme, and is currently writing her second, *A Tram to the Beach*. Both novels explore contested territories. Michalowska is Director of The Wapping Project.

RICHARD SENNETT is a sociologist, musician and Theatrum Mundi founder, and currently serves as Senior Advisor to the United Nations on its Cities and Climate Change Initiative. He is Senior Fellow at the Center on Capitalism and Society at Columbia University and Visiting Professor of Urban Studies at MIT. Previously, he founded the New York Institute for the Humanities, taught at New York University and the London School of Economics, and served as President of the American Council on Work. Over the course of the last five decades, he has written several books about social life in cities, changes in labour, and social theory.

SANTIAGO CONFALONIERI is a Uruguayan creative and graphic designer. He is interested in the different actors that influence contemporary society and is passionate passionate about collaborative and interdisciplinary projects addressing different aspects of art, culture, and education, in order to generate different discourses and alternative ways of inhabiting society. He is currently working at Villalba Studio and studying Visual Communication Design at the Universidad de la República in Uruguay.

Theatrum Mundi
c/o Groupwork
15a Clerkenwell Close
EC1R 0AA
London, UK

Theatrum Mundi Europe
59 Rue du Département
75018
Paris, France

w: theatrum-mundi.org
e: info@theatrum-mundi.org

Editors: Cecily Chua, Labeja Kodua Okullu and Marta Michalowska
Concept: Cecily Chua
Design: Marcos Villalba, Santiago Confalonieri
Proofreading: Imogen Free, Sriwhana Spong
Copy Editing: Cecily Chua
Printing: Grafiche Veneziane
Typeface: Gravity and Marist (Dinamo), F Grotesk (Radim Pesko)
Research Team: Andrea Cetrulo, Cecily Chua, Elahe Karimnia, Fani Kostourou, John Bingham-Hall and Justinien Tribillon
Illustrations: Cecily Chua

Image credits © Cecily Chua, 2023

Theatrum Mundi is a European centre for research and experimentation in the culture of cities with a mission to help expand the crafts of city-making through collaboration with the arts, developing imaginative responses to shared questions about the staging of urban public life. Based in London and Paris, Theatrum Mundi works through performance, design, publishing, research and teaching, with partners across Europe and the Mediterranean.

Theatrum Mundi is a registered charity N° 1174149 in England & Wales and association N° W751251542 in France.

Friends of Theatrum Mundi
see theatrum-mundi.org/membership/

Nick Tyler (TM Patron)
Joao Villas
David Chipperfield Architects
Rudi Christian Ferreira
Catherine Visser
Central Saint Martins

Printed and bound in Italy

ISBN: 978-1-3999-4017-7

Colophon